HEY
YA!

ST. MARTIN'S GRIFFIN
NEW YORK

HEY YA!

THE UNAUTHORIZED BIOGRAPHY OF OUTKAST

CHRIS NICKSON

www.stmartins.com

BOOK DESIGN BY AMANDA DEWEY

Library of Congress Cataloging-in-Publication Data
Nickson, Chris.
    Hey ya! : the unauthorized biography of OutKast /
      Chris Nickson.
        p. cm.
    Includes discography (page 201).
    ISBN 0-312-33735-3
    EAN 978-0312-33735-3
    1. OutKast (Musical Group) 2. Rap musicians—United
States—Biography. I. Title: Unauthorized biography of
OutKast. II Title.

ML421.O98N53 2004
782.421649'092'2—dc22
[B]

2004050946

First Edition: September 2004

10 9 8 7 6 5 4 3 2 1

TO GRAHAM SHEA, THE WONDERFUL SON I LOVE.

May you live long and prosper, but above all, may you have
a life filled with happiness, and unblemished by sorrow.

CONTENTS

HEY YA!

INTRODUCTION

SOME PEOPLE like to play by the rules. Others make their own rules. The really creative ones throw every kind of rule book straight out of the window and do whatever they want.

Most of the time that doesn't work the way they'd hoped, and it can take years, maybe even centuries, for people to catch up.

But sometimes, just sometimes, someone hits it right. Then they don't just ride the wave, they make the wave, and they're riding on top of it.

Welcome to the world of OutKast.

Since 1994 they've been laying a new path for hip-hop, and from the very start they've been successful. Even their first single, the funky "Player's Ball," with its shoutouts to their native Atlanta, topped the *Billboard* Hot Rap Singles chart for six weeks. Their debut album, the dizzily titled *Southernplayalisti-cadillacmuzik*, turned platinum. And they've been building on that ever since.

They've followed their noses, followed their muses, followed their hearts. They've pulled from funk, R&B, old school hip-hop, New Wave, rock, jazz, soul, and anything else they've wanted—and mashed it up.

Every album they've released has gone at least platinum—a million copies sold. *Stankonia*, released in 2000, more than tripled that. And the real breakout, the one that launched them into the stratosphere, *Speakerboxxx/The Love Below*, is currently over nine million and counting. And let's not forget the six Grammy Awards that Andre 3000 and Big Boi have taken home over the years, either. Or the MTV Video Music Award, the BET Award, the American Music Award, the World Music Award, and that first Source Award in '95.

They've done it all by sounding like absolutely nobody else. No West Coast G-funk or East Coast bling-bling on their records. With OutKast, the Dirty South hasn't just risen again, it's taken over.

"There's a lot of quote-unquote hip-hop acts today, they stick to beats and rhymes, and we really like to experiment and play with a lot of different elements of the music. We keep it exciting, and I guess that's where the weirdo funk comes in."

Does that explain why "Hey Ya!" topped virtually every chart in existence? Or why it's the most downloaded ringtone for cell phones? Or that "The Way You Move" nestled underneath it at number two for weeks before taking over the top spot for another six weeks? What they've been doing, they've been doing right.

There's no formula to OutKast. They're the hip-hop band

that's not hip-hop, the rappers who are so much more than rap. And that's exactly what's helped the duo of Andre 3000 and Big Boi become so popular. Just when you think you've got a handle on what they're doing . . . it changes. They've grown, and with each record they've found a new audience, unlike so many others who started at the same time and have spent the last decade doing retreads of the same old clichés.

"Rappers say, 'I'm keepin' it real,' but then four or five albums down the line they're keepin' it the same real," Andre objected. "You can't be keepin' it real if you don't grow."

These days their audience is only partly from hip-hop. Thanks in large part to the wonderfully bizarre "Hey Ya!," the people who listen to them cross every possible demographic. You like Prince? It's in there. Jazz? That, too. Funk? Step right up. It doesn't matter if you've just discovered OutKast. It's better late than never.

They're so hot that they have the next two years fully mapped out. There's a film in the works, a "sophistifunk modern-day Renaissance musical," the soundtrack of which, of course, will be the next OutKast album. Then there's the disc that will celebrate their ten years of recording. Big Boi's already been touring alone—hitting the road is something Andre hates—and his pit bull kennel is doing great business, even registering a new kind of pit bull, the rare blue.

Andre, meanwhile, is realizing the Hollywood dream he's harbored for a few years (and which led to his half of *Speaker-boxxx/The Love Below*). He's set for a role in *Be Cool*, the sequel to *Get Shorty*. There's even talk of him playing legendary guitarist Jimi Hendrix in a movie—no bad choice, since there's a strong facial similarity.

In other words, there are no peaks. If you're OutKast, you

just keep on climbing. That's what you can do when you've thrown out the rules.

Big Boi and Dre (as people call Andre) have grown up together. They've matured together. They're not idolizing the things that most people will never have: the gold and jewelry, the huge entourages, and the Escalades. And they're not preaching, either.

"Once you start getting preachy, that's when you start being like an overbearing parent," said Big Boi. "We just giving you everyday life as we see it."

And obviously, a lot of people see it the same way. Not many other hip-hop stars have been shouted out from the electoral campaign trail—at least, not positively. But when General Wesley Clark (a man not known to be down with the bass) was running for the Democratic presidential nomination, he could comment on the rumored breakup between Dre and Big Boi: "I don't care what the other candidates say—I don't think OutKast is really breaking up. Andre 3000 and Big Boi just cut solo records, that's all."

He was right, of course, and that's what *Speakerboxxx/The Love Below* was: two solo discs under one name. But they worked and complemented each other. And propelled by the unprecedented success of "Hey Ya!," which was named single of the year in so many polls, it went mega. "Hey Ya!" was so big it even received its own parody at the start of *The 2004 Golden Globe Awards* show. It was simply *that* recognizable. For a while you couldn't turn on your radio without hearing it.

It's the ultimate vindication for the duo who style themselves as the poet and the player. But like any labels attached to OutKast, those two fall off very quickly. Maybe once it was true, but they've long since gone beyond any kind of image. These days they just are . . . and what they are is whatever they want to be. And like everybody else, they're not just one thing. They're parents (Dre had a child with singer Erykah Badu, while Big Boi is the father of three children who live with him), celebrities, but everyday people, too. They run businesses— they own apartment complexes, apart from everything else—in addition to OutKast. They're the grown-ups who'll never completely grow up. They might be mature, but they're still also the two kids who hooked up because they were into hip-hop and were both "a tad bit different."

Where others have spent albums praising the thug life, Out-Kast's messages have always been more positive. Dre might have had his brief period as a wannabe gangsta when he was a teen, but you won't find glowing references to hos and Glocks on their albums. They're a lot more conscious in their flow, not even afraid to speak their political minds on songs like "B.O.B." (or "Bombs Over Baghdad," to give it the full title).

And unlike so many other rappers and producers, who are only interested in the last beat, they've kept their ears open throughout their career. They both grew up listening to a lot of different music, and now they embrace even more. They're not afraid of the new—they welcome it with wide-open arms.

Maybe it's because Atlanta's never been quite the same as other Southern cities. It's set squarely in Georgia, and it's proud of its Southern heritage, but it's also had aspirations of being a big cosmopolitan city. It's a place of business and commerce, moving away from its past. It's a vibrant city, where the Atlanta Underground is a huge attraction to the thousands who visit each year.

At the same time, compared to the East and West coasts, it's remained a little bit country—and proud of it. But for a long period it—and virtually everywhere except New York or L.A.— was off the map for hip-hop. If the South was known for anything musically (apart from country), it was for the bass music from Miami. Everyone wanted to be from the coasts. In the Atlanta clubs, people would yell out loud for New York in the house, but stayed strangely quiet when asked if Atlanta was in the house. It just wasn't a cool place to be from.

And now it is. Building on the success of TLC, Xscape, and Goodie MOb, OutKast has raised the bar. Because of Big Boi and Dre (and maybe another local product, Ludacris), Atlanta, the South, and the drawl are what everyone wants. But as Big Boi pointed out, it doesn't really matter where you're from— we're all going through similar stuff. Be proud of your roots, but be aware of the world.

"It's just from another part of the globe. Everybody's going through the same thing, just about. Only thing that'll change is just where you from. Because [hip-hop] music is all the same; ours just reflects the Southern lifestyle."

Well, maybe it did once. And somewhere deep inside, that's still there. But it more accurately reflects the OutKast state of mind than their state of the union. After all, these days, while Big Boi is still in Georgia—in Fayetteville, where he has his house and business, a dog kennel—Dre is mostly a West Coaster, out in sunny Los Angeles. At least, that's the geography; when he's making music, his mind might be in outer space (and maybe it has been, if you listened to the science-fiction and inner-journey obsessed *ATLiens*).

For all that their first three albums each topped the million mark in sales, and their singles "Player's Ball" and "Elevators (Me & You)" topped the rap singles charts and hit the Top 40, most people didn't even have OutKast on their radar until *Stankonia*. And that was in spite of a blowup with civil rights icon Rosa Parks, over the track named for her on *Aquemini*. That ended up before the Supreme Court—making OutKast probably the first hip-hop band to be featured in the highest court of the United States—and remains unresolved.

With *Stankonia* it all began to change. Going multiple platinum and spawning a number-one single in "Ms. Jackson," suddenly OutKast had an audience that went well outside hip-hop and into pop. It was also when the awards really began flowing, and a performance at the 2002 Grammys made people sit up. There was something very different—and very weird—going on in hip-hop.

You could say it all paved the way for *Speakerboxxx/The Love Below*, but that's not right. Each OutKast disc is, as Dre said, "a time capsule." The next one might build on the last, but they exist individually; there's deliberately no continuity. Big Boi and Dre have learned from what they've done, but they never repeat it. *That* would be too easy. And when you've thrown out the rules, "easy" no longer applies.

There's a sense of adventure, even of danger, in listening to an OutKast track. You feel that even they had no idea where it would go when they started it. They haven't so much pushed the envelope of hip-hop as torn it completely open. To even label it as hip-hop anymore doesn't do it justice. In the older sense of the term, OutKast are making pop music, always daring, and sometimes—like "Hey Ya!"—absolutely sublime. No wonder *USA Today* called it "a universal home run that comes along once in a decade, once in an artist's career."

The only thing is: OutKast doesn't see "Hey Ya!" as a peak. To them, the song is just another step on the way. The best is yet to come, and the chances are that it'll be totally unexpected.

"Our influences are so vast that if we drop something, you better believe it's going to be groundbreaking."

1. OH, ATLANTA

TO UNDERSTAND OutKast, you have to understand Atlanta and the South. Because that's what shaped the band.

More African-Americans live in the South than anywhere else in the United States. Beginning a century ago, there was an exodus of blacks to the North, especially to cities like Chicago and Detroit, which offered greater opportunities and wages—and an escape from the blinding prejudice that existed widely in the South at the time.

The North, with its cities and industries, was seen as the future, a place of hope, while the South was viewed as backward and even degrading to African-Americans. That lasted into the civil rights era of the 1950s and '60s. Many blacks lived in the country, farming as sharecroppers, where they could barely make a living, or just scuffling by at other jobs. There were shining exceptions, of course, but for most life was hard—and sometimes dangerous. It's no surprise that the South, specifically the cotton-heavy Mississippi Delta, gave birth to the blues, which, along with jazz and gospel, was the African-American musical form for so many years.

Times do change, and progress happens. By the 1970s, after a Georgia peanut farmer named Jimmy Carter became president in 1976, the image of the South was changing. The South became the Sunbelt. Retirees from the North were attracted by its climate and cheaper cost of living. Industry and commerce began moving in, too, to take advantage of the abundance of labor available—and also the cheaper cost of doing business.

Atlanta was the hub of the South. It was smack in the center of the Southeast, the biggest city around. Yet it was also quite accessible to the East Coast, especially the Northeast, where there is an intense concentration of finance and commercial institutions. Atlanta began to grow like crazy. Major companies opened offices there. The airport expanded, becoming one of the busiest in the world. The city was refurbished in grand style as a cosmopolitan city: a business and shopping Mecca.

It was a new Atlanta, a new Georgia, a new South. And that changing world was the one into which both members of Out-Kast were born in 1975.

Antwan Patton, known to everyone as Big Boi, is the elder, but only by four months. He was born on February 1, while his partner, Andre Benjamin (Andre 3000 or just Dre), first opened his eyes on May 27. Although they'd eventually meet in Atlanta, neither of them began life within the city limits.

For Big Boi, Savannah was home. Situated on the Atlantic Coast, Savannah is a historic city, the home of the nation's oldest

African-American congregation: the First African Baptist Church on Montgomery Street at Franklin Square. Some of the city's buildings date back as far as the 1700s.

Antwan was the oldest child in the family, followed by four younger brothers and sisters. His mother, Rowena Patton, was still young when he was born, while his father, Tony Kearse, was in the Marines; he'd eventually rise to the rank of sergeant, although he died in 2003.

It wasn't an easy existence, raising four children on not a lot of money, and for all its charms, Savannah didn't offer a lot of opportunities. When he was young, Antwan had other responsibilities besides his studies and taking care of himself; as the eldest, he had to look after his siblings, too, a heavy cloak to throw on a child. In an interview in *Blender*, he stated there were widespread substance abuse problems among the adults in his family, and that he, his siblings, and his mother lived in a Motel 6 for a year.

"We used to live off bologna sandwiches from a cooler," he said. "I've been to the lowest low." And in the family there were "drugs and alcohol, domestic abuse—crazy shit."

Antwan had the usual dreams and desires of every boy. Sports offered a way out of a poor lifestyle, and despite his size, he thought about becoming a professional football player. After all, they were the stars, they made the money, they were the heroes. But Antwan was also a good student, a young man who looked forward to attending college in the future. The way the mind worked fascinated him. Possibly because of the size of his family and the amount of time he spent around his brothers and sisters, he considered training to become a child psychologist.

Whatever he thought about, Antwan's ideas were a little outside the box. No matter what, he was determined to make something of himself. Interestingly, though, music wasn't in his plans, at least when he was young. That would come a little later.

While Antwan was finding his way around Savannah, Andre was growing up in Decatur, which was, to all intents and purposes, a suburb of Atlanta, located between downtown and Stone Mountain. Named for Stephen Decatur, an American naval hero in the War of 1812, the city still has the comfortable feel of a small town. Andre was an only child, the son of Sharon Benjamin (now Sharon Benjamin-Hodo), and Lawrence Walker. The couple split up while Dre was still a child, and he lived with his mother, who worked on the assembly line at General Motors. It was good, well-paid work, and she bought a house for the pair of them in one of Atlanta's burgeoning suburban subdivisions. Her rules for Andre were strict, and she expected him to obey them, which the self-confessed "mama's boy" did for a long time.

Dre's aspirations to become an architect fell through because "I didn't like math." But one thing Andre did love was music, and from an early age he exposed himself to a lot of it. Not just blues, gospel, soul music, and early hip-hop, although these were a big part of his education. Dre listened to *everything*.

Georgia was a state that enjoyed a remarkably fertile music scene. James Brown, the godfather of soul, was from Macon and still lived there. Macon had also been the home of one of soul's greatest vocalists, the late Otis Redding, who died in a plane crash in 1967 at the height of his fame. And in a completely different direction, the college town of Athens was the bedrock of an alternative rock scene in the first half of the 1980s, as R.E.M. catapulted from local to national stardom. Dre surely was exposed to these styles and more as he skipped around the radio dial.

But rap was the new style, with pioneers like the Sugarhill Gang, Kurtis Blow, and Grandmaster Flash among the artists who popularized the new music. It was a revolution, one that would literally change the course of music history. Rap grew from a combination of things: reggae, blues, funk, and the bragging of "the dozens," the kind of top-that insults that had been around for generations in the African-American community. The music behind the voices was new, too. Using a pair of turntables and a mixer, skilled DJs culled beats, bass lines, and melodies from older records, working the vinyl into a seamless flow that was a backdrop every bit as important as the rhymed raps themselves. Originating in the Bronx section of New York, rap exploded on record.

It all went into Dre's melting pot. But rap music was his first love. It was inevitable because he essentially grew up with it. Very verbal and articulate, with a quick mind, Dre made a natural rapper. But his ideas extended far beyond words. To him, music was a whole, not segmented the way the industry tried to make it with divisions between pop, rap, soul, and so on.

By the time he was in junior high, Andre was writing say-no-to-drugs raps with a friend, T-Bone. Together they listened to Eric B. and Rakim, whom Andre called "an inspiration." But that ended when T-Bone moved away from music and into sports.

Both Dre and Big Boi were raised in the church, which meant getting dressed up every Sunday and attending services. It was one of the foundations and certainties of life for them. And it was also exposure to another kind of music, the gospel music heard in Baptist churches: jubilant, soulful, and often ecstatic. More than anything, though, church offered a spiritual underpinning that's remained a part of their lives, one that Dre has speculated separates Atlanta music from other areas, as so many kids grew up in the church, singing in choirs. And there was also the weight of history around them.

Dre noted that "Atlanta was one of the last places to get out of slavery, and so that striving and sense of struggle comes across immediately in our music."

By the time he was a teenager, Big Boi was getting into music, too. For Antwan, it was the P-Funk of Parliament and George Clinton that blew the roof off, along with Run-D.M.C., one of the major rap acts of the time, the first rap group to cross over to a rock audience with their remake of "Walk This Way" along with the song's originators, hard rock band Aerosmith (the song that helped revitalize Aerosmith's career). If Big Boi hadn't cast his net as wide as Dre, that was just because he'd discovered music later. But Big Boi became hungry for music. After his family moved from Savannah to the East Point area of Atlanta, he went to the free concerts in Grant Park, lapping it all up. He was especially turned on by the deep '70s funk of the Ohio Players. "You just wanted to get up there and jam," Big Boi remembered.

When he was fifteen, Andre began to resent his mother's strict rules and moved out of his mother's house to live with his father in Atlanta. This put Dre in the East Point area of the city, Big Boi's neighborhood, a far cry from the laid-back atmosphere of Decatur. The idea was that his father would instill some discipline in him; instead, he found himself in a bachelor house with few or no rules and began running a little wild for a while.

For his sophomore year of high school, he was about to enroll at Tri-Cities High School. Just coincidentally, that was where Antwan—whose nickname of Big Boi came, ironically, because he was small—happened to be a student.

It was a relatively new school, opened in 1988–89, with a catchment area from the Tri-Cities areas of College Park, Hapeville, and East Point. There were two main areas of study at the school: college preparatory and career technology.

The Tri-Cities area is predominantly African-American, with wages well below the national average. Many of the people in the area are employed in lower-paying service jobs. Many of the students live with a single parent. A fairly large school (in 2003 it boasted over two thousand students), it is a school that takes pride in boosting its pupils academically; in fact, the home of the Tri-Cities Bulldogs received an Inspiration Award in 2003 as America's Most Improved High School.

Even when he started at Tri-Cities, Dre refused to fit easily into any pigeonhole. He was smart, into music, but he was also into things no one would have expected: skateboarding and BMX bikes. The one thing he wasn't into was school. After his father dropped him off at school in the morning, Dre took off around the corner every chance he got.

Although they were in the same class at school, that wasn't where Big Boi and Dre met. They probably knew each other's faces, but the first time they actually spoke was in Atlanta's Lenox Square Mall, where they both happened to be shopping— window-shopping, because neither of them had the money to buy clothes. It was outside the Ralph Lauren store, where they were looking wistfully at the fashions.

From the very first, there was a bond between them. The young men were a little outside the norm, not so much refusing to conform as not even thinking about it.

"When everyone was wearing Starter pants, we were wearing flower print shorts," explained Andre. "We were just a tad bit different."

According to Big Boi, though, "We were preps. We wore loafers, argyle socks, and V-neck sweaters with T-shirts. We were new to the school and we didn't know anybody."

In hip-hop, they were all about bands like Poor Righteous Teachers, KMD, Leaders of the New School, De La Soul, Brand Nubian, and A Tribe Called Quest, who colored outside the lines—and managed it quite successfully. That was a far cry from the booty-shaking music most of the kids in school were listening to. And Antwan went even further. His uncle had introduced him to the music of English singer-songwriter Kate Bush, which moved him in a way he couldn't explain, so "I'd sit and think and play her records for hours."

Both Andre and Antwan wanted to hear the newest beats, so they'd go down to Five Points Flea Market on the weekends to buy mix tapes with the freshest stuff on them from Ron G, a New York DJ.

In so many ways, they were complete opposites.

"They've always been very different people," commented Dre's mother. "You could start by saying Andre is the introvert and Big is the extrovert."

But they came together on music and clothes—clothes that didn't fall into the lines of fashion that everyone else was wearing. Instead, they tried to be individual and stand out.

"We thought we were pretty fly as far as clothes in high school," said Dre. But even more important than image was music. They often sat and watched videos together, eventually deciding that they could do a lot better rapping than most of the rappers they were seeing on television. The first time they actually rapped together was at Big Boi's aunt's house. One of them started and the other picked it up "every four or six bars." Since their talents meshed so well together, the natural thing to do was form a band. That was what they did, naming it 2 Shades Deep—a name that didn't last too long, as there was already an R&B group called Four Shades Deep. They then briefly became the Misfits, until they heard of a punk/metal band with that name. So they searched for something different, a word that perfectly described being outsiders. With a little help from the dictionary, they found exactly what they needed.

"We came across the word 'outcast' and just kept the pronunciation key spelling of it," explained Andre. And OutKast was born.

Soon they'd walk around each other's kitchens, rhyming and practicing. And it wasn't too long before they were ready to go public with their skills, at an open mic night at Club Fritz, a place in Atlanta's West End. However, the club "had only one Korg mic, with a short-ass cord," said Big Boi, "so we'd pass it back and forth, trying to catch each other's word and pass the mic."

It went well, which set up more open mic nights. But although music was a huge focus for them, it wasn't all-consuming at first. Antwan was doing well at school, with a 3.68 GPA and plans for college. Academics were his way out. His dream of being a child psychologist was still very much alive.

The rapping and writing was strictly part-time. But that doesn't mean it wasn't serious. They were also listening to everything coming out of the local hip-hop scene; they wanted to know their competition and their peers. They weren't impressed by what they heard—there was simply no originality about any of it. The producers were all following the trend of putting together tracks in the East Coast style, which was the fashion. The beats were a little jazzy, the bass lines a little lighter. It worked if you were A Tribe Called Quest, who'd helped break that ground, but it didn't speak to Georgia.

Where was the Georgia red clay soil? Where was the soul that crept down from Memphis or the funk of James Brown (except in some of the sampled beats)? There was a whole history of African-American music waiting to be explored, and everyone was ignoring it. Almost everyone just wanted to be big, to be tougher than the rest, rather than to be creative. Dre and Big Boi listened and realized that it didn't compute to them.

By 1992 they had their rhymes together, and their ideas were taking shape. What they didn't know was that elsewhere in East Point were a few other guys who also had a vision for hip-hop.

Rico Wade, Pat "Sleepy" Brown, and Ray Murray loved the music. Unlike most people, though, they didn't want to be on the mic. They didn't have the skills or the flow to be rappers. Instead, they used their ears and imagination. Hip-hop had moved from a pair of turntables and a record collection to writing beats and using samples—snippets of other tracks taken and brought into a new creation. Sometimes they were played with digitally, to the point where they were unrecognizable, sometimes they were used straight. But the people who created the tracks were every bit as important to the new music as the rappers themselves—they just stayed more in the background and didn't get all the glory or celebrity. But they were responsible for the sound, people like the Bomb Squad, who worked with Public Enemy, or Dr. Dre out on the West Coast. They shaped the whole feel of hip-hop.

While making the tracks was fine, the sound men needed a rapper on top. And if they were doing something fresh, they didn't want a rapper who was just ripping off another style. They needed someone with originality to match theirs. The difficulty was finding that someone. Taking on the production name of Organized Noize, all they could do was keep working—and keep searching.

In 1989 Atlanta was beginning to enjoy a musical renaissance. Kenneth "Babyface" Edmonds and Antonio "L.A." Reid opened LaFace Records—the name was taken from their nicknames. The pair already had an enviable history. As part of the soul/funk band the Deele, Edmonds and Reid had enjoyed several hits, in addition to writing chart successes for other artists like Pebbles and The Whispers. When they relocated to Atlanta, Babyface's career as a solo artist took off (he'd released his first solo disc in 1986), and his *Tender Lover* spawned four hit singles—not a small feat at all. His successful solo career helped make him a power in the industry and lent a higher profile to the young label, which had a deal with the major Arista label. Edmonds and Reid hadn't forsaken songwriting for their new business venture. In fact, the Midas touch was still very much with them as they penned smashes for Bobby Brown, Sheena Easton, and others.

Although they had a label in Atlanta, Edmonds and Reid took their time signing new acts, going for music they thought would work across the country. Their first major signing was R&B singer Toni Braxton. Her first single, "Love Shoulda Brought You Home," was a hit right out of the box in 1991, and from there she never looked back. Neither did LaFace. They signed acts like Jermaine Jackson, brother of Michael and former member of the Jackson 5, and the female trio TLC, who were Atlanta natives and the first local signing.

The other big player on the Atlanta scene was Jermaine

Dupri. While not yet in his teens, he'd performed on stages with Grandmaster Flash, Run-D.M.C., Whodini, and Cameo. He began working as a producer at the age of fourteen in 1987, when he not only produced, but also got a record deal for the band Silk Tymes Leather. Two years later Dupri had his own production company: So So Def. In 1991 he saw two boys performing at an Atlanta mall and signed them. That was Kris Kross, whose single "Jump" stayed on top of the charts for weeks, as did their debut album. Now with his own So So Def label, distributed by the giant Columbia, Dupri produced a couple of tracks on the TLC debut, before finding another all-female group in town, Xscape (whose alma mater was Tri-Cities High). They performed at Dupri's eighteenth birthday party in 1991 and two years later were looking at their first platinum album, *Hummin' Comin' at 'Cha.* He also discovered hard-edged female rapper Da Brat and helped give her a massive hit with the single "Funkdafied" (and the album of the same name).

So Hotlanta was really starting to happen in black music and a vital, if more underground, rock scene. Two of the staples of what would become the burgeoning jam band trend—Col. Bruce Hampton and Widespread Panic—were both Georgia-based.

Having things brewing could have made it easier for Big Boi and Dre, but none of what they heard was hitting them to the core. They knew what they wanted to do, what they could do. But they didn't have the studio ability to make it happen. They needed people with that expertise to hook up with and make complete bomb tracks.

The pair of them were into fashion—at least, their interpretation of fashion, which was outside any mainstream. And part of fashion has always been the 'do. The hair is as important as the clothes. And that meant investment in hair products. Not just shampoo and conditioner, but more specialized items. And that, in turn, meant trips to the beauty supply store.

Rico Wade of Organized Noize was making ends meet by working in one of those stores: Lamonte's Beauty Supply. Andre and Antwan walked in one day; an ex-girlfriend of Antwan's knew Wade. The conversation turned to music. Wade learned that they were rappers, and they heard about his beats. While every kid on the block wanted to rap, there was something about these two that intrigued Wade enough to invite them to audition for him.

Big Boi and Dre were more than ready. Hanging with them was a new friend, Big Gipp, who was part of Goodie MOb, another new band. Big Gipp had his car with him, an Isuzu Trooper, and they all piled into it. Big Boi and Dre put on the instrumental version of A Tribe Called Quest's "Scenario" and proceeded to freestyle back and forth for the next seven minutes. They didn't care about any hooks or choruses; they were simply flowing. Wade was impressed by what he heard—impressed enough to invite the pair over to his basement studio, aptly called "the Dungeon." It wasn't an inspiring place. All the equipment was secondhand, some of it old. The basement itself was completely unfinished, the floor Georgia red clay, with dust everywhere. The only furniture was some beat-up patio chairs; if you wanted to sit, there were the basement steps. But, rough as it was, it was the laboratory of Atlanta hip-hop.

Down in Wade's basement, they waited to hear the music, probably not expecting much creativity. But "from the first time

Rico pressed 'play' on the tape, we knew we had our producer," Antwan said, "because the beats were like nothing I had ever heard before."

The rhymes surprised Wade just as much, too. This wasn't the tired old bragging or the clichés. This was different, with its own flow and a style that just screamed Atlanta, right down to the drawl. It didn't owe anything to the East Coast or the West Coast of Dr. Dre and the N.W.A. posse.

It was a given. They all had to work together. And from the first meeting, they knew they were going toward something very special. Now that they had a focus, a goal, and the right people, they were ready to jump into it.

That meant spending a lot of time at Wade's crib, not just hours, but days in the basement working over material. Big Boi and Dre would be there the whole night sometimes, sleeping on the floor, writing, listening to beats, and working on ideas. Nights became days as they started to skip school.

Dre was less academically motivated than his partner, but his mother still wanted him to get his diploma. And since Big Boi was carrying a good G.P.A., there was no way *his* mother was going to let him throw that away. Once the first rush of working and hearing something different wore off, Antwan realized he didn't want to give up his education, either. In fact, the young men's parents wouldn't let them sign the contract they eventually landed with LaFace until they turned eighteen.

"I finally realized that school was something I needed just as much as music, and I didn't want not having a certain piece of paper to hold me back," Big Boi said emphatically.

By now they were juniors, exploring life more, not legally adults, but feeling like it. Dre was even hanging with the gangstas for a while.

"I do remember Dre in a Cadillac with a Glock, getting high, waiting for niggas to run up," remembered his cousin Angelo. But it was just a brief phase, thankfully, and about to pass.

Antwan stayed in school, but Andre dropped out after eleventh grade. It wasn't a popular decision at home—and maybe not even a wise one, but he did it. There was still a wildness in him that wasn't ready to calm down, and he had to go his own way. He worked jobs he hated to have a little money and spent all his free time in the studio. After their first album came out, Dre did go to Washington High Night School to obtain his G.E.D.

Having access to a studio was a major luxury. Around the country, most aspiring rappers had to hustle and do whatever they could, by any means necessary, to afford studio time. Here they could record whenever they wanted, and they took advantage of it. There was lots of work to be done, and plenty the teenagers could learn from the older producers. In fact, Antwan credited Organized Noize's Ray Murray for bringing him along as an artist.

"Ray . . . taught me how to rap," he explained. "I was a writer, and he just showed me things about being an MC. It was more mental than it was showing me specific things. We call him the Yoda."

Even as they were working with OutKast, the sound men in Organized Noize were looking for other projects. They were in contact with labels around town, other producers, and other acts (which would include Goodie MOb). They couldn't put all their eggs in one untried basket. Besides, their abilities were wide-ranging, and they were ambitious. They wanted outlets for the music in their heads. They were hungry and ready to hustle. Like everyone else who was struggling, they were hunting for that big break.

But Andre and Antwan were special to them. They were all tight, and there was a musical bond. Together they could just let their imaginations rip and create something unique. Everyone wants a new sound for their music, but not usually so tweaked that it sounds weird. The OutKast guys, though, were up for anything and everything. Big Boi and Dre spent long hours working at the Dungeon. But so did plenty of other rappers.

"There'd be nine, ten guys and everyone would take turns rhyming over a beat," recalled Big Boi. "It would be your turn to rhyme, and you'd start, and then Rico'd be like, 'Oh, did the pizza come yet?' Break your fucking heart, man. There was a shed out back. That's where I got into some Luke Skywalker shit. I'd sit out there for hours at a time, no music, just writing."

Finally it began to happen for Organized Noize. After a lot of local productions, they came to the attention of LaFace Records, who'd just put out the first TLC album, produced by Dallas Austin, Jermaine Dupri, and De Funky Bunch—all proven talents with strong track records. The label was wanting remixes of some tracks, though, and for those they could afford to take some chances. In fact, it was a good idea to use unknowns for remixes, where imagination and creativity counted.

Maybe it would be the big break, maybe not. But it was the biggest thing to have happened to Organized Noize, and they were all over it. Remixing is an art in itself, and it's not uncommon for big-name producers to be paid literally tens of thousands of dollars to rework a track. The remix is better described as a reinvention. The track is stripped down, and often only fragments of the original are used—a vocal line, a bass line, or a hook. Everything else is built from scratch until the finished product becomes entirely different. It can be aimed at the dance floor, the chill-out room, or anywhere. The possibilities are infinite. It becomes a work of the producer's imagination, not the artist's.

When there's a lot riding on a piece of work, you give it a huge amount of attention, and that's what Wade, Brown, and Murray did with their assignment. It had to be perfect, it had to flow, it had to sound good—which wasn't always that easy, given that they didn't own a state-of-the-art studio. But they not only knew their equipment, they knew how to use it creatively, how to get sounds out of it.

Finally it was almost done. The track was there, except for one thing—it needed some rapping. And who else were they going to call but OutKast? They were comfortable with them, knew what they could do, and knew they could do it right. This was a huge leap for Dre and Big Boi. After months of working on demos, this was a vault into the big time, a finished track that was going to appear on disc. For them all, this could be a stepping-stone to the big time. Organized Noize knew exactly what they wanted, and worked with OutKast until the disc was perfect. Take after take down in the Dungeon, long hours, but worth every second when they heard the playback and then the final mix.

After they gave it to the label, everyone was flying—but full of fear, too. What if they didn't like it and kicked it back? What if they just thought it was terrible? Just as in life, you didn't get many chances in the music business. Blow it the first time and there might never be a second.

So when the word came that it was accepted, there was a celebration down in the Dungeon. Organized Noize (and OutKast) were going to have a record.

———————

It was the start of the rise of Atlanta. In addition to huge hits for LaFace, Georgia rap had arrived on the national scene, thanks to Arrested Development. They mixed up funk, soul, and blues on "Tennessee," which broke out across the country. On their debut CD, *Three Years, Five months and Two Days in the Life of . . .* they offered positive messages as an alternative to the negativity of gangsta rap. It sold well, with its Southern-fried grooves and deliberate country attitude. To many people, it was one of the most important hip-hop albums of the early '90s. It certainly showed that there was a market for rap that was outside the accepted mainstream. Record buyers were willing to take chances as long as the music was good.

This was something the executives at LaFace realized. And they were looking out for new talent with that ability to hit home all over America. Listening to the TLC remix by Organized Noize, everyone was struck by the rapping. It could have been good luck—or it could have been real talent. There was only one way to know for sure, and that was to hear more of this duo called OutKast.

When Kawan Prather, director of artists and repertoire (the department responsible for signing and developing new talent) for LaFace called, Dre and Big Boi were bouncing. But it was still very far from a done deal. There was no contract yet. First the label wanted to listen to the demos they'd done with Organized Noize.

Those went in, and then they just had to wait. Every day without a call—a call either way—was like an eternity. They just dragged by, making work and school almost impossible. Going in and trying to record was out of the question.

And then Prather called. Could they come in to the office?

The news wasn't what they'd hoped. The label wanted them to perform a showcase, to hear how they sounded onstage. So, backed by a DJ, Dre and Big Boi played in a club. They thought they sounded fine, but the people from LaFace weren't as convinced. In the end, LaFace passed on the band, not because Out-Kast wasn't good, but because they didn't think OutKast was quite ready yet.

Nobody was happy to be turned down by a hometown label, but Dre and Big Boi weren't about to give up. They believed in what they were doing and the sound they were creating with Organized Noize. They contacted other labels, and Polygram asked them to showcase. Attracting the interest of a locally based label was one thing, but catching the eye of one of the big national labels was a different league altogether. LaFace had money and the backing of the Arista label, but Polygram was a major player, too.

That showcase didn't work out either, but by now a buzz about OutKast was starting to go around. It was looking good for the future, although they'd all hoped that the future would come right now.

Then, when they were least expecting it, they received another call from LaFace. Could they come back into the office?

"PLAYER'S
2. BALL"

THEY CAME into the office and listened. And they walked out with their dreams come true—they had a record deal with LaFace. They were both barely out of high school, and their world had blown up in a way they could only have hoped for and dreamed of.

Antwan might have been college material, but given a choice between making a living rapping and going to school, it wasn't even a contest. And for Andre, music had consumed him for so long that this was simply the ultimate.

"When we first got our deal, we was happy as hell! We just wanted a shot and L.A. Reid gave us that shot. It wasn't even so much about getting paid, because I think the advance was like fifteen grand. We were kids, so to us, that was great. That was gonna set us straight for a minute and give us a chance to go in the studio. We didn't have to work our regular jobs anymore."

To a pair of eighteen-year-olds, even in the age when athletes and rappers were making millions, $15,000 was a lot of money. It would have been easy to get a little crazy, but both Dre and Antwan were focused on the music. And they were working with Organized Noize, who wanted to make the most of this— and were going to make sure they worked.

And work they all did. The hours down in the Dungeon grew even longer. They'd always felt like a lot had rested on the demos they made, but it was nothing compared to the pressure of this. This was real. This was their debut. They had a lot to say, and they wanted it to make a huge impact on the whole hip-hop scene. It had to stand up and represent Atlanta when everyone was hollering New York and the West Coast. OutKast was nothing if not ambitious.

There was pressure on the guys in Organized Noize, too. They were the producers, and the deal was through their production company. They had to come up with the dopest beats to make people pay attention.

Dre and Big Boi might as well have moved into the Dungeon, they spent so much time there.

"Everybody lived there," recalled LaFace's Prather. "We slept on hardwood floors for a year. There wasn't a weekend during that first year that we all weren't over there. We were grinding. It was, like, by any means necessary."

It was highly unusual for a label's A&R man to spend so much time with an act. That said a lot about the way the label viewed OutKast; their investment was much more than money. They sensed the immense potential and wanted to make sure it was explored. There was something different going on, but hugely commercial—if it was done right. They just wanted to be sure everyone stayed on track.

Nothing was rushed. They signed in 1993, and it would be nine months before the first single would appear. That gave them time to work and to refine everything. Ideas were suggested, tried, and rejected. Others worked and were developed.

One thing everyone agreed on was the sound. It had to be Southern, with the soul and funk that was part of the air down there. That was something the East and West coasts just could not duplicate; they didn't feel it the same way. Even the G-funk out in L.A. wasn't the same thing. Music wasn't in the earth the same way out there.

It helped when Arrested Development blew up, and Rap-a-Lot Records had been representing Houston since '86. They'd hit big with the Geto Boys, whose "My Mind Playing Tricks on Me" turned from an underground to an overground hit in 1992, one of the most original hip-hop tracks to date, just creeping with gangsta paranoia. Apart from that, and the bass music out of Miami, the South was very quiet. OutKast was going to change that.

It wasn't just that the Southern music was different. The Southern style of rapping had little to do with New York or L.A. Snoop Doggy Dogg actually helped set the stage for Southern rappers by affecting a drawl when he was introduced on Dr. Dre's *The Chronic*, then on his own *Doggystyle* in 1993. People were ready to hear something more laid-back.

Making the album was an exercise in adventure and compromise. The label was paying Dre and Big Boi to follow their vision. But they didn't want OutKast to follow it so far that the results were uncommercial. It had to be original, but recognizable enough to sell in the national market. That made for an interesting balancing act, especially for a pair of eighteen-year-olds who were just straining at the leash. If it worked, the results could be huge.

Neither Andre nor Big Boi were really street kids, even if Dre had hung with the gangstas for a little while. But they wanted a record that was street-oriented. They came "from the generation where samples *are* hip-hop," as Big Boi noted, but Organized Noize didn't work that way. They programmed the beats, but they liked the particular feel of live instruments, especially keyboards, bass, and guitar because they make the music more real and immediate. It wasn't a throwback to the Sugarhill Gang school of the early '80s. The music funked, it echoed from studios like Alabama's Muscle Shoals, where so much classic soul had been recorded, or Memphis, where blues and soul came together on Beale Street. They wanted music that was deep, but still as greasy as good barbecue. And you could only do that with real people playing in the studio. It was about feel as much as the notes anyone heard.

This was going to be more than just a way of introducing a new band. This was going to be a statement about life, about being black, and most definitely about the South, and specifically Atlanta. And they were going to do that without being anything close to Arrested Development—OutKast's vision was much more urban, based in the big city. They could be now while referencing the past. They didn't need to sound deliberately rural like Speech and his posse.

Arrested Development hit big, then imploded very quickly. It was an object lesson in how things could go so right and then so wrong. But Dre and Big Boi were too tight and had too much to say to let something like that happen.

Through the second half of '93 they worked. Days, nights, it didn't matter if they were focused on something, getting the flow for a track. Even as they were pushing ahead, they were refining their skills, getting the flow down, and bringing in other ideas from soul, funk, and R&B.

"We did like thirty-something odd songs," Dre would recall a couple of years later, "and we cut it down to a tight thirteen, fourteen cuts. Some of our tightest rhymes and beats. We got Goodie MOb on the album. I mean, it's just a whole collaboration between Organized Noize, OutKast, and the whole family, man."

The coasts were about the gangstas, the playas, the money, and what it bought: the gold chains and the Benzes. That just wasn't the reality of life in Atlanta—at least, not the life Out-Kast and the life that people they knew experienced. Yes, there were drugs around, just as there were everywhere, especially weed, and they weren't going to deny it. But instead of talking about driving a Lexus or a Mercedes, reality was a Cadillac cruising on a Saturday night through the 'hood. It wasn't drinking Möet, it was grabbing a soft drink or a forty at the 7-Eleven. Food was wings or popcorn chicken, the stuff real people ate.

All of that and more was going to be reflected on the track LaFace selected for the first single. "Player's Ball" was the whole album encapsulated in one track. It shouted out the neighborhoods OutKast and Organized Noize knew all too well—College Park, East Point, and the areas around them—and injected some Curtis Mayfield soul in the falsetto singing on the chorus.

Releasing it was taking a huge chance. Atlanta was out of the loop, it wasn't cool. It was hick, country. But maybe the time was right—and thanks to the success of Babyface, TLC, and

Toni Braxton, LaFace was becoming a real force as a label. And Atlanta *was* making a musical impression nationally, thanks to Arrested Development and Jermaine Dupri's productions. Maybe it was time to put the city on the map.

The single was an irresistible piece of slow funk that harked back more to the slow jams and quiet storms of '80s urban radio than hip-hop. And when Dre slid into that falsetto, it was impossible not to sing along. The song had melody, which had been missing from too much hip-hop for too long. The accent was Southern, but not too much—the drawl was like honey, warm and inviting. There was a groove, but it never overpowered. Edward Stroud's guitar with its wah-wah sourced funk, from *Shaft* to Johnny "Guitar" Watson, but softly. And the supple bass work from Preston Crump was never static; this was a track that rolled.

"Player's Ball" was originally intended as a Christmas release, even though its vibe was anything but seasonal. It had more to do with warm weather than with the holiday season. In fact, the original mix included sleigh bells, although once it began getting radio play, the band was asked to remove those—which they did. It really started to catch in February 1994, thanks to a lot of radio play and heavy promotion.

Like every song that could blow up, it needed a video, and "Player's Ball" got one. Interestingly, it didn't come out of Atlanta connections. Thanks to L.A. Reid, who knew everyone in the business, copies of the single had gone to people in New York, and it caught the ears of a then-unknown Sean "Puffy" Combs, who invited them up to the Big Apple to open for his act, Notorious B.I.G.

Working with Notorious B.I.G. was serious big time, and they were all over it. While they were there, Puffy offered to direct the video for "Player's Ball," which was an offer they couldn't turn down.

Combs came with a strong background in the music business, with his experience as a record label executive at Andre Harrell's Uptown Records, but the video turned out to actually be fairly generic—as hip-hop videos went. It did, however, feature Caddies and not imports, and it captured some of the laid-back Southern vibe that helped make the song stand out. The bottom line was that it was presentable, and it didn't rock the boat by being strange—and the video definitely helped the song.

By March "Player's Ball" sold half a million copies and topped the *Billboard* Hot Rap Singles chart for an incredible six weeks. This was exactly what LaFace Records had been hoping for, but it was still way beyond the wildest dreams of OutKast. This was big time, this was real. Dre was still eighteen, Antwan barely nineteen, and OutKast was number one. But there was a lot more to come. The single *really* took off with Freaknik.

Freaknik was something that was specifically Atlantean. While many white college kids headed to Florida or California for spring break, African-American college kids flocked to Atlanta to party. It's a tradition that no longer exists, but when it happened, students turned the city upside down for a week. It was loud, it was a party, and sometimes it got seriously out of control. If you were under twenty-two, you were in it. Kids drove around town, partying in the clubs and on the streets. Sometimes there were fights with the police (one of the reasons the city finally put a stop to Freaknik), and there was always plenty of excess.

In 1994, when thousands of kids descended on Atlanta for Freaknik, "Player's Ball" was the soundtrack of the party. It was the perfect fit. It was a party record, a celebration, and it simply *was* Atlanta. Sales of the single spiked sharply. The timing was perfect, too, just before OutKast's first album would hit the stores. So while the college kids were spending their money on "Player's Ball" and singing along as they drove, they could also jam with *Southernplayalisticadillacmuzik* on the car stereo. And they did.

In the wake of Freaknik, as the kids headed back to colleges all over the South and the Northeast, they took OutKast with them. By the end of April, "Player's Ball" cracked the Top 40. At the time, making the Top 40 was like searching for the Holy Grail. With a few exceptions, rap had yet to make a massive, regular impact on the mainstream singles chart. To land there was to break out from the ghetto and into the mall. Big Boi and Dre did it on their first time out.

It was important, though, that OutKast made people understand their definition of a player, which was a little different from that of most people's.

"A player is somebody who can take care of they business in the game, the game of life," Dre explained in *Source*. It wasn't just about playing the women.

"You can be a regular, average Joe and be a player as long as you handle your business," said Big Boi, going further. "If you're true to yourself and true to what you're doing, then can't nobody call you out."

It was obvious that OutKast had made an impact on the country with their hit single. But it wasn't easy to represent Atlanta nationally. There were still a lot of people who didn't think that hip-hop from anywhere else besides New York City or L.A. could be taken seriously.

"People thought that the South basically only had bass

music," said Dre. "At first people were looking at us like 'Um, I don't know.'"

The sales figures could speak for themselves, and they were loud. By June of 1994, *Southernplayalisticadillacmuzik* had sold a half million copies, and OutKast and Organized Noize had a second gold disc.

They were going to get paid, that was for sure. But Dre and Big Boi also needed to make sure they handled their publishing, which was an important component of the business. There was more to it than simply putting out a record and hoping that it sold enough for royalties to start coming in (and for many artists, they never did—not just because of sales, but because every dollar of the advance had to be paid back, plus costs of promoting a record, and many other things). The publishing rights, which were the royalties coming to the songwriters of a song, were often more lucrative than record royalties. And in their naïveté, they hadn't even thought of the rights.

While "Player's Ball" still ruled the rap singles charts, OutKast was approached by Chrysalis, who managed to sign the band for a relatively small publishing advance. The young men didn't splash out too heavily on jewelry or cars—Big Boi treated himself to a new Lexus, while Andre settled for a 1990 Cadillac. Mostly, they were investing it in their musical future.

At the Dungeon, all the original recording equipment had been secondhand; it was all the guys in Organized Noize had been able to afford. But it did the job. Much as they liked working with the crew, OutKast wanted the freedom to be able to work on tracks by themselves—and Organized Noize was already busy with other projects, like the debut from Goodie MOb, who'd also signed to LaFace. Dre and Big Boi hit the music stores and bought all the same gear they'd used in the Dungeon, then other things they thought might help them develop their sound. It wasn't flash, but it made sense. Having hit it straight from the word "go," they knew there was a future in music. They also knew they hadn't even begun to scratch the surface of what they were capable of doing. It would take time and a lot of work. They weren't turning their backs on anyone; they were learning: about music and about themselves. They knew they had a long way to go. Gold records were just the start of a creative process that was beginning to unfold.

"Player's Ball" wasn't the only single to come from the album. Both the title cut and "Git Up, Git Out" were issued, but neither managed the same success. The latter stood as a total contrast to "Player's Ball." It was a serious, inspirational track built around a small funk groove featuring Cee-Lo from Goodie MOb. It was an exhortation for people to actually do something with their lives, rather than letting life pass them by while they just got high. In an example of dropping knowledge, they even mentioned "Get Up, Stand Up," the anthemic song by Peter Tosh that had been one of the centerpieces of the stage act not only for Tosh but also his reggae colleague, the iconic Bob Marley. While OutKast's song was much more street-oriented, the message was exactly the same.

Crime wasn't the way, the song said; any kind of crime, whether it was pimping, selling weed, or running numbers. And there were shoutouts to Organized Noize and L.A. Reid in the song because they had given OutKast the opportunity to make the most of their talent. But the bottom line was that they'd made the effort to do something. You had to look outside the everyday if you were going to get paid. And you had to vote if you wanted a voice.

And, of course, it was an Atlantacentric track, like virtually everything on the album was. They were proud of their home—including the fact that it was going to host the 1996 Olympics.

Like virtually everything on the record, there was guitar all over it, which was enough to set it apart musically from the rest of hip-hop. The guitar was so important to Southern music, from the blues onward, that you couldn't have soul without the guitar, you couldn't funk without jammin' on one. And "Git Up, Git Out" paid homage to the South in its bluesy vibe while doing its best to get people off their butts to make a difference—even if it was only in their own lives.

Entertainment Weekly gave it an A grade, praising it as real Southern hip-hop, with its "casual funk" and positive messages.

Of course, it could have been seen as an irony that these two teenagers were saying this—especially as one of them had dropped out of high school, and they were both barely old enough to vote. But it's never been about how old you are, but about how wise. And across the seven and a half minutes of "Git Up, Git Out," Dre and Big Boi showed that they were wise beyond their years. They embraced the music and the rhymes and showed they had something to say that went way beyond the party vibe. They were speaking to African-American kids like themselves, and they knew exactly what they were talking about.

It was a killer cut, but it was probably doomed from the first. With a message that encouraged listeners to get involved with life rather than escape in drugs, it just wasn't chart material. But in the context of the album, it really stood out.

Southernplayalisticadillacmuzik was the real deal. If "Player's Ball" had been an appetizer, this was the full seventeen-course meal. It took plenty of chances—three of its tracks ran over six minutes, and another four stretched more than five minutes. There were little interludes that seemed to interrupt the flow of the music, but actually offered illustrations about life in the South.

All of a sudden this version of hip-hop was offering a credible alternative to the music coming out of the East and West coasts. The Dirty South was in the house—and proud. Many of the tracks mentioned Atlanta, either by name or by its neighborhoods. It was a record that didn't bow down to fashion, musically or lyrically; it celebrated it roots loudly. This was life down in Hotlanta, laid out for everyone to hear.

What they were saying was important. Unlike so many rappers, whose idea of keeping it real involved talking Benzes and the kind of goods most kids would never to be able to afford, Dre and Big Boi kept their reality very real and on the East Point streets. It wasn't just talking about what they knew and saw—although that was a big part of it—it was that they'd never had the money and didn't even have the desire for the same kind of luxuries. They were down home, where a tricked-out Caddy was cool and chicken wings were what you ate when you were driving around.

Yes, drugs were mentioned, several times, but those were simply a part of life everywhere in America, not just in Atlanta.

There's more to any hip-hop record than *what* you say. There's also *how* you say it, plus the sound that's going on behind it. These factors are equally important.

Andre and Antwan had their own flows. Dre was more chilled, laid-back, and happy to slip into some singing any time at all. Antwan was more hyper; his words skittered out in gun-bursts, eager and devastating. Both of them were obviously from the South; at the time a few people even said they had difficulty understanding them because of the accents. There was a melody in the way they spoke, however, that made everything flow easily. They were so tight that picking up from each other was natural, creating a unity that worked even in their contrasts. It was fresh, it was different, and it was dope.

So was the work of Organized Noize. The innately Southern feel of the music was ultimately down to them. Some people would even believe that OutKast's success was really down to the production rather than their own skills—which said a lot about the quality of the production. Organized Noize defined the sound and expanded it, with lots of greasy Southern funk underpinning everything. The beats had more to do with soul than hip-hop, and so did the guitar and organ that were the foundation of many tracks. There was a lot of church in there, with hints of Sunday morning gospel sessions in the music. But at the same time George Clinton and P-Funk could be heard, Al Green, Curtis Mayfield, and the backbeat of Memphis's, Stax label (provided, of course, by the venerable Booker T. & the MG.'s). It was retro, but it worked—and it was subtly updated. When the guitar took off and splashed an extended solo all over "Funky Ride," it was straight off Funkadelic's mothership, with no boundaries, and it roared.

And that was why the partnership of Organized Noize and OutKast was so good. None of the young men wanted limits; they wanted to explore their imaginations fully. These baby steps didn't go that far, but they were definitely meant as only the first steps: discovering their sound and playing with it. It's worth bearing in mind that it was a debut for them all, and they were still a little tentative about how far they should and could go. After all, they wanted to carry people with them. If the first leap had been too great, no one would have followed. Taking it in stages was fine.

The fact that *Southernplayalisticadillacmuzik* sold a half million copies really spoke for itself. No, it wasn't millions, but it wasn't bad, either. It was a foundation on which they could build. They'd put Atlanta hip-hop on the map (since Arrested Development had fallen off) and showed that the South still knew how to get funky. The door was open; now they all had to keep on walking.

For Organized Noize, the success of the disc helped them with other projects. They were working with Dre and Big Boi's friends in Goodie MOb (the name is actually very conscious, meaning Good Die Mostly Over bulls**t), whose own debut would receive wide acclaim. And they'd cross over into R&B to work with TLC on *Crazysexycool*, then soul—a natural fit—to head into the studio with Curtis Mayfield, a giant of soul music who'd been paralyzed when a lighting rig fell on him. Curtis was coming back with an album called *New World Order*, and Organized Noize was helping with the production. As if that wasn't enough, they had their own deal for a side project called Society of Soul, who were getting ready to unleash their only disc, *Brainchild*. They'd gone from hustling to the fast lane—all on the strength of one album.

Antwan and Andre were enjoying the ride that came with success, but their heads weren't being turned by it. They might have been a couple of kids, but they'd grown up fast, and their mothers had kept their feet firmly on the ground. They were getting paid, and Big Boi knew that "you can still play and have fun, but don't take the money for granted." Just because there was cash in the bank now didn't mean there would be in a few years—this was a fickle business.

The young men knew they had skills, but they had to keep working and developing them. They had a hot album and people were interested. But they both knew that they could do a lot better. Neither of them was about to rest on the laurels of their success. Dre and Big Boi went straight back into the studio— their own this time—to work on new material and to learn exactly how to get the most out of it.

That didn't mean they no longer wanted to work with Organized Noize. They were just more ambitious in terms of the overall sound. By knowing how to use their new studio, they could do more with their ideas and bring more to the party in a creative sense when they properly recorded next time. That next time was coming a lot faster than they'd imagined.

The pair were signed up to provide a song for a new movie, *Higher Learning*. Written and directed by John Singleton, who'd been responsible for the seminal *Boyz N the Hood* and *Poetic Justice*, it was a film that dealt with racism and problems on a fictional college campus. With people like Laurence Fishburne, Ice Cube, Tyra Banks, and rapper Busta Rhymes, it looked to be quite high profile; being on the soundtrack was prestigious. Certainly there were other big names on there—Ice Cube, Tori Amos, Brand New Heavies, and Rage Against the Machine, among others—pretty much covering the spectrum of non-mainstream music.

It was a shame, then, that the movie didn't do well. But every little thing helped get the OutKast name out more.

Given that people on the coasts had been so down on Southern hip-hop, it was a surprise for OutKast to find themselves nominated for Best New Rap Group in the Source Awards. *The Source* was one of the main magazines covering the music, and its name carried plenty of cachet with fans. Whether they expected to win or not, it was (as the cliché goes) an honor to Dre and Antwan to even be nominated. It was recognition that they were doing something right and that people really appreciated their work.

What really was surprising was that, in January 1995, OutKast walked away with that award. Inside a year they'd gone from being nobodies to the best new act out there. They'd had a top single and an album that had gone gold and was still selling. They really were going places. The partnership, which was only four years old, was paying off big time.

It was also respect for what the musicians down in Atlanta were doing. They were all creating a new sound. OutKast was just at the head of the pack; many others were coming. But the award was the biggest boost their career could have had at that point, and it was reflected by the fact that in just three more months, *Southernplayalisticadillacmuzik* roared through another half million sales to break that magic million barrier and go platinum. And that was a major achievement, well beyond anything any of them had even dared to dream about.

But what do you do when you achieve your dreams right away? Andre and Antwan had dreamed about being given a chance to go into a studio and lay down their rhymes. Organized Noize gave them that. Then when they heard the sound, they'd dreamed harder, for a record deal. LaFace came along. Then for a hit single and an album that people listened to and bought. They had all those—and now the acknowledgment of people who judged the business.

Simple economics meant they couldn't just stop and say they'd done it all. The royalties on a million albums, even on the publishing side, was nice money, but it wasn't a stake for a lifetime. And if you were ambitious, you kept going, because you knew you could be even more creative, that you could take it further. Big Boi was twenty, Andre nineteen—they had many years ahead of them. There was a lot still to learn about life, and plenty of wisdom to impart on record.

What they'd really done so far was build a very solid foundation. Now they were going to be taken seriously. And by not spending their money foolishly, they were looking toward the future. When they went out on tour, there was no huge entourage with them. The people who came along were all there for a specific reason, and it was a no-frills tour, with people sharing rooms. They knew the difference between the art and the business.

When the money did come in (and there's always a lag of about a year before the royalties begin), they invested it in bonds and real estate, buying apartment buildings in Cartersville, Georgia. That was the stuff that was going to grow and keep them solid long after their rapping days were over. The music wasn't a means to an end. The music was about the music. But it didn't hurt to look after tomorrow as well as today—something far too many rappers—indeed, musicians of all kinds—have forgotten once the paycheck arrives.

One of Big Boi's investments sounds unusual, and it probably did come from out in left field. He opened a dog breeding kennel in Fayetteville, Georgia—the town he moved to when all the success began, although Atlanta remains a base for him, too. The kennel, called Pitfall Kennels, specializes in pit bulls, the breed that seems to be favored by most rappers and hip-hop fans, to the point where pit bulls have become completely associated with the music. He insists that, unlike their image, pit bulls are actually friendly dogs, less likely to bite than many other breeds. This could be seen as an exercise in vanity, except for the fact that Big Boi takes a great interest in the business, which is run on a day-to-day basis by his brother James, who is younger than Big Boi. It is a serious business, with the puppies selling from anywhere from $1,200 to $2,500, and it's even advertised in the booklet for *Speakerboxxx/The Love Below*. He'd also become a father for the time of a daughter, Jordan. He apparently wasn't married to her mother, and didn't live with her, but his son lived with him.

If there was one problem with *Southernplayalisticadillacmuzik*, it was that there wasn't enough in the subject matter to set it completely apart from other rappers who were around. Yes, it was about the street, and what happens on the street is pretty much the same from city to city. But there was also ample evidence from tracks like "Git Up, Git Out" that OutKast had much more to say than passing street messages.

"A lot of people got the message of our first album mixed up," Antwan asserted. "They just heard 'Player's Ball' and thought it was all about the pimps, the cars, and all that mess." There was a lot more going on, but you had to listen closely to hear it, something most people weren't willing to do. But the young men were still in the process of finding their real voices—

which was another reason for equipping their own studio, where they could take all the time they wanted and needed to develop.

There was more coming.

Having hit it big, they had to play some live dates, which was a very different proposition from being in the studio. Big Boi loved it, Antwan didn't. For most of its life, hip-hop has been far more a recording format than a live one. The flow works better on disc, where the sound is clear. Onstage, all too often the P.A. is messed up and making out the words becomes impossible, especially in larger venues. The beats and backing are prerecorded, as the era of the DJ and the turntable has largely passed. And very few acts have been adventurous enough to bring live instruments onstage to back them up.

Big Boi and Dre survived the dates, but they really wanted to be at home, where they could work on something new. They were ready to build on their success and take a quantum leap, not just for themselves but for hip-hop. Let the other rappers rehash the same old same old; OutKast had plans.

The question was: How far were they willing to push the envelope? If Andre was any indication, the answer was pretty far out. He'd taken to wearing turbans and dressing strangely. The young men had always had a unique take on fashion, but Dre was heading way, way out there. It certainly set him apart, but this was just plain weird, to the point where people began to wonder about him. He also became a vegetarian, and the thoughts about weed and guns and gangstas had become things of the past. But what would Dre do with it all, apart from showing it as style?

Success meant there was a lot resting on what OutKast did next. But success also meant they had plenty of time to work on a follow-up. They could vanish into the studio, alone or with

Organized Noize. If a record didn't appear until the middle of 1996, that was fine.

The best strategy was to ignore the pressure and make the music that was in their hearts. There's a difference between art and commerce. Commerce chases the dollars, while art exists for its own sake. OutKast might have started out as a way to get paid, but that had quickly changed. Now it was all about the art, taking it to the next level. Dre and Big Boi didn't need to keep it real on the streets. They needed to keep it real in their heads and hearts, to get out all the stuff that was inside, no matter what it was. If it sold, that was great. The studio wasn't the real world; it was a fantasy land where they could go wherever they wanted—and they did.

OutKast had time, and the young men used it constructively. The party time was over. The future was calling them, and they were ready to embrace it.

It was fun in the studio, but it also took hours, days, weeks, and months of very hard work. As anyone who's ever tried to write and perform a rap can tell you, it isn't easy. It's about the rhythm, and the flow, making the rhymes inside rhymes work. There's an art to it. It needs inspiration to write it, but it needs a lot of sweat, too, a lot of editing and time to make it work properly. Doing that with two people, no matter how close they are, complicates things further. Working all that around the beats, the effects, the sounds, and samples is like putting up a building. OutKast had to plan it all out carefully. There was luck involved, but also communication, and going layer by layer, floor by floor, until it was finished. And often they never really knew exactly when it *was* finished. They had to stand back, say enough, and let it go, move on to the next track.

OutKast was part of the Dungeon family, which helped the young men a lot. They could play stuff for other people, get criticism and advice, and help. They could draw on other people to help them out, to fill out a cut—or even run it, if that was what was needed. It really was like a family, there to support each other, and Big Boi and Dre were the star brothers, although there were more coming up fast behind them.

3. ALIENS

LAFACE GAVE Andre and Antwan a lot of freedom. The record company was in the music business and sought commercial success, but Edmonds and Reid, but also believed in their artists and allowed them the freedom to go where they wanted musically.

But going your own way in a business that likes the safety of the formula can be very dangerous. It's all too easy to leave an audience behind, especially when you decide to leave boundaries out of the equation, which was exactly what OutKast had done in the studio. They weren't really reinventing themselves; they were beginning to grow into the people they'd become. They were still young enough to dive headlong into it and push it out all the way, without half-measures.

"We just wanted to keep the thing going and give our peers and the people who listen to us something new to feed off of," said Dre. "Then they can come back and do something innovative that we can feed off of to keep the whole thing going."

The young men were tired of hip-hop all sounding the same. So OutKast decided to give it a serious punt into the future. Dre and Big Boi expanded their listening even more, taking in everything from the classic rock of Led Zeppelin and the alternative sound of Stone Temple Pilots to the smooth, sultry pop of Sade and the roots reggae of Bob Marley. Nothing was out of the question.

If they had a model, it was George Clinton's Parliament/ Funkadelic crew. Their space-age P-Funk, combining some very funky playing with Clinton's often bizarre lyrical ideas, a completely oddball sense of humor, and some great musicians, had stood out in black music during the 1970s and '80s. Sometimes it had been better received by white audiences, as he mixed up black music—Clinton's roots were in the doo-wop of the 1950s—with rock, jazz, and anything else he heard that he liked. The result rarely achieved massive sales (with the exception of a few singles like "Atomic Dog"), but found a great deal of critical acclaim and influence. Their stage shows, with UFOs and silver costumes (sometimes homemade), were an amazing sight—and musically explosive. When Clinton sang about tearing the roof off the mother, he had the goods to do it. He also made sure that he didn't take everything too seriously, that he kept a healthy sense of fun in his music. That stopped it all becoming too serious—music, after all, was meant to be enjoyed.

That was certainly the attitude OutKast was taking into the studio. Anything went, anything was possible. If it was in their imaginations, it could happen on record. And if they could be as funky as Funkadelic, they'd really be hitting something rare.

Many casual hip-hop fans were not familiar with George Clinton's music—or if they were, it was just through samples. So Dre and Big Boi were introducing a spirit and feel that was fresh to their audiences. Besides, Clinton's music was simply a jumping-off point for OutKast to build on.

Hip-hop had finally begun to crack the suburban market. Born in the ghetto, it had graduated and crossed over to become part of the mainstream rather than an alternative. In large part, that was due to Dr. Dre and his protégé, Snoop Doggy Dogg, whose albums had all been multiplatinum and unleashed a much broader wave.

For those suburban audiences, less educated than city folks in the nuances of the styles, the differences between East Coast, West Coast, and Dirty South didn't matter so much, as long as it sounded good.

With "Player's Ball" and their first album, OutKast had inadvertently kick-started a national trend toward tricking out Caddies and Monte Carlos around the country, as people bought up old models—which were fairly cheap—buffed them up, put on low-profile tires and wide rims. The fact that they guzzled gas was a sense of pride; it meant you could afford to run them. People spent thousands of dollars customizing their vehicles and making them street-ready.

So there was an audience outside the hip-hop core that was into the music—and ready for something new. The real hip-hop heads, the connoisseurs, understood what was good and what wasn't. But at the same time, they were a little more set in their ways about what constituted the music. Progressive hip-hop had never had a big audience among the traditionalists. It might get great reviews, but the sales were outside the usual market. De La Soul was a perfect example. The Long Island threesome released their debut, *3 Feet High and Rising*, in 1989 to massive acclaim from critics. But its blend of soul, psychedelia, and everything else they could lay their hands on appealed to people who would never normally buy a rap record, not the hard-core base of fans and artists. And the band was eclipsed by the rapid rise of gangsta rap in the early '90s. De La Soul went from the front of the hip-hop pack to the back of an appealing and colorful dead-end street.

But the situation had changed. Different kinds of music had begun to bleed into each other, and hip-hop was bigger than it had ever been. People had open ears in ways they'd never had before. All of these factors were falling into place to help Out-Kast along the way.

It certainly helped that OutKast had established a solid base among the real hard-core hip-hop fans and artists. It offered the kind of credibility money couldn't buy (all you had to do was think back to the appalling pseudorapper Vanilla Ice to understand that). They weren't even coming up out of the underground, not with a platinum album to their credit and a hit single a lot of people knew.

Whether they realized this themselves at the time, or even thought about it, doesn't matter. They had a vision, and they were going to pursue it, even if it was commercial suicide.

Being creative extended to samples, too. On their debut Out-Kast and Organized Noize had established a studio ethic of using beats and a lot of live instruments, in sharp contrast to so much hip-hop, which was sample driven. Dre and Antwan liked their samples, but they weren't about to steal tracks (in fact, there's only one obvious sample on their second disc, from the

Curtis Mayfield song "Danger, She's a Stranger"). They weren't into remaking older songs. What they did was sample sounds, then run them through processors, so by the time they ended up on a track they were completely unrecognizable. That worked well, because it kept a good original flavor to the music, and also meant that, since they weren't taking from other records, they didn't have to pay royalties to other artists for the samples they used.

While OutKast was in the studio, out in the real world hip-hop was staying stagnant, with the same old tired gangsta rhymes coming out over tracks that were almost starting to sound generic. There were only a few real artists out there telling it with style and thought, like Tupac and Notorious B.I.G., along with Snoop. Those were the big three at the beginning of 1996, and in just over a year two of them would be gone, in crimes never solved that simply added fuel to the ongoing feud between MCs on the East and West coasts. The South stayed out of that loop—and was better for it. Dre and Big Boi weren't interested in rivalries; there was no future in that or a gun culture. Making music was what they were here to do, and they were going to keep on doing it.

Even before they dropped their second album, in August 1996, there were plenty of rumors floating around about Out-Kast. Dre's eccentric style of dress, in particular, had people saying he'd gone over the edge. People didn't understand why he wanted to dress in turbans and weird clothes; it didn't make any sense. The man had money, he could afford what he wanted, and he was dressing like he was crazy. Some people even thought that maybe he was gay. For the first time, but certainly not the last, there were suggestions that OutKast was breaking up.

So what if Dre dressed strangely. None of that was going to

affect his rhyming skills. What he had done was grow up and develop his own, highly individual perspective on life. Antwan was growing up, too, although he seemed far more grounded in the real world: a parent, a dog breeder, a man who was still a player once his business had been taken care of. Dre and Big Boi were like left brain and right brain. And like the mind, OutKast needed both sides to fire properly.

No one's ever discussed what the executives at LaFace said when they were presented with *ATLiens*, the new album. The chances are good, though, that they were taken by surprise. It was hip-hop, but . . . where it was going was a different matter altogether. It seemed to have more in common with George Clinton's mothership in its science fiction ideas than any kind of street reality in the South. But, full credit to LaFace, Edmonds and Reid went ahead and accepted it.

LaFace even took the ideas for the artwork, which was, essentially, a comic book—a very bizarre one at that. It starred Out-Kast, with Organized Noize cast as freedom fighters and L.A. Reid cast as a kind of android. The dark powers were censorship and control of the population, which had to be brought down—and Atlanta itself was the lost city of Atlantis.

It was odd stuff indeed, but certainly no stranger than the music. No one knew more than the LaFace brain trust the chance they were taking with this disc. If it didn't fly high, it was going to sink OutKast completely. But this was the record Dre and Big Boi had wanted to make, and they were happy with it. The alternative for LaFace was to turn it down and send the young men back to the studio. Then more rumors would fly, and it would be another year before any product would be ready for release. It had already been more than two years since "Player's

Ball" and *Southernplayalisticadillacmuzik*. If LaFace waited much longer, the world might not even care about OutKast anymore.

ATLiens was a record that's often been criticized as incomprehensible, but there were several commercial tracks on it. Taken out of context, there was no reason they couldn't be hits. As was standard practice, the album was preceded, in July 1996, by the first single, "Elevators (Me & You)." It sounded so completely different from anything else out there that the single immediately stood out. And, most important, the song had a great chorus and hooks. It was apparent that OutKast had been doing a lot of work on their craft in the last two years. Not only were they better in the studio, they were more comfortable just being themselves and they'd really improved as songwriters and rappers.

LaFace readily acquiesced to OutKast's choice for that first single, and sent it out to radio and to stores. Influenced by dub, the Jamaican reggae style where instruments dropped in and out of the mix and plenty of delay was the main effect, it was a spare track underneath the flow of the voices. The chorus referenced family and Cadillacs—family because it was important, the center of everything, and Caddies because they were still the vehicles of choice in the Atlanta 'hood. But it lurched from line to line—and that was its hook. "Elevators (Me & You)" was a summer song with a joy; it was very frankly autobiographical in its content, which added to its appeal.

Obviously a lot of people agreed, because it not only ran straight to the top of the *Billboard* Hot Rap Singles chart, but also the Hot R&B Singles chart, where it stayed in the pole position on both for the next four weeks. Like "Player's Ball," it also cracked the main Top 40, establishing OutKast as an act that was really happening. They were doing it on their own terms, and people were still listening and buying.

While the single was flying high, the album arrived. Really, "Elevators (Me & You)" was the perfect precursor for the whole CD. It was twisted enough to give a clue that people would be hearing something really out there. Like all real artists, Dre and Big Boi were putting themselves and their reputations on the line. The first album had been a warm-up; it still owed a lot to other people. But this was definitely them.

So it was gratifying when, within a month, *ATLiens* topped the *Billboard* R&B Albums chart for two weeks, just as "Elevators (Me & You)" went gold. By November the album was platinum. There were probably huge sighs of relief at LaFace, too, as everything succeeded—in fact, *ATLiens* would eventually sell a million and a half copies, building on what OutKast had achieved before. Considering the fact that Andre and Antwan were both only twenty-one, their continued success was remarkable. Not so much for the sales figures, but for the chances they were willing to take—and their true development as artists.

As hip-hop went, it broke every mold. It played to the alienation of youth, of the South, and of OutKast—even their name indicated that Dre and Big Boi stood outside it all.

"Being an alien is just being yourself, when people don't understand you," said Andre, who was misunderstood himself by so many in and out of the industry. "We just trying to let everybody know there's a place for everybody in this world. You just gotta find yourself and be true to yourself. That's how you get prosperous and happy."

All of a sudden, they were role models and seemed quite happy in the position. They'd moved from the daily concerns of rap to something much deeper, something that could have invited laughter if they hadn't been so serious about it. They were still very much of Atlanta, and of the South, but they'd come to realize they were a part of something much bigger—the world itself. And if they could help kids who felt the way they'd felt, then they were saying something. Very interestingly, the messages on the album were positive. They knew what life was like on the streets, but there was more to life than the streets— there was a life inside, too. They might not have been as mystical as P. M. Dawn, whose almost New Age hip-hop had topped the charts a few years before, but they were traveling to places rap had never gone before—and a lot of people were coming along for the ride.

ATLiens wasn't an easy album. It demanded a lot of the listener. But it gave a lot back, too, both in new beats that startled and lots of fun and funk. To sit and hear the whole thing in one sitting took an effort—and not only because there was a lot to digest. To most hip-hop fans, it was too strange, too different.

From its neo-soul introduction (that also offered a nod to the '60s pop group the Lovin' Spoonful), it launched into the killer cut of "Two Dope Boyz (in a Cadillac)" that took their laid-back Southern funk ten steps further than on their debut and also introduced the aliens concept. But less than three minutes in, it cut off, heading into the infectious title cut. That pushed up the Southern factor and the lyrics showed that OutKast wasn't taking itself too seriously—Big Boi and Dre were happy to subvert a lot of hip-hop clichés, but over a rich backing, with some new beats.

There was a lot of autobiography in the rhymes, to be found in snippets here and there. But there was also a philosophy. And it became apparent as the album unfolded that there was an ethic to the whole disc. Dre pointedly disavowed guns, alcohol, and weed, which was a relatively controversial stance for a hip-hop MC. On *ATLiens*, the soulful funk of the backing was more developed and integrated with the voices. Thanks to some concerted work, the young men were now really sounding like themselves, kicking it on the groove of "Jazzy Belle" or the hit single.

But by "Ova Da Wudz" it was obvious that something different was going on, with its spooky vocal sample and jazzy bass line and the rap going in strange directions on the chorus—as opposed to the very real life of the verses. That was a pattern, contrasting the grit of everyday life—without glamorizing any of it, the way so many rappers did—with the alien idea, to show how so many were really outsiders. It was a sophisticated concept for a rap album, a theme that recurred often, not least on the surprising "E.T. (Extraterrestrial)." In what might have been a first for hip-hop, it was a song with no beats, maybe the first ambient hip-hop track. To many, that was astonishing enough. It broke a basic rule of the music, where the beats were so important. Yet, by breaking the rules, OutKast, made the song stand out, made it memorable. And so it worked and drew even closer attention to the words—which was the intention, although they admitted they simply hadn't been able to find beats to work under the floating melody—and it was that melody that dictated the flow of the rhymes.

Though it was out there, the real progress was in the way Dre and Big Boi used the flow of the words. It was most obvious on "Elevators (Me & You)," where the chorus seemed to stop and go, but it was also apparent in "Babylon," where the pronunciation of each word was deliberately staccato, giving an odd effect—but one that wasn't immediately obvious, before heading into R&B/gospel territory. There was a subtlety to the art here.

"Mainstream" was an ironic title, as the cut was anything but. With a gentle groove that suggested the Isley Brothers's version of "Summer Breeze," the pair traded off each other and still kept the creamy feeling of old school soul.

Dre shouted out Decatur on "Decatur Psalm," where there really were no boundaries. Wah-wah guitar straight out of '70s soul, percussion, effects, female backing vocals, horns, and dub delay showed that Organized Noize had come a long way, too. It was probably the best backing track in hip-hip since the Bomb Squad had started working with Public Enemy, almost a decade before. Who cared if it was one of the least commercial tracks on the record? It was also one of the best, bursting with creativity, on the mic and behind it, with the devil in the details and the details on display—if you listened closely. And OutKast wanted you to listen carefully. This was entertainment, but it was also a lot more on a deeper level.

"Millennium" boasted one of the oddest choruses ever—one without words, which might have seemed strange for a rapper, for whom words were the stock in trade. But it worked, over a female speaking. Just weird, with a lazy groove behind it, and a guitar playing. It made a good lead into "E.T. (Extraterrestrial)," with blacks as the aliens of mainstream America—and OutKast even more outsiders than any of them, trying to teach and advise. Other artists like Poor Righteous Teachers had taken on similar roles. They'd been praised for their work, but they'd never found a big audience; it's a fine line between teaching and preaching.

OutKast started off "13th Floor/Growing Old" with a poem, another daring move, before diving into the song. It was stripped down, beats and piano—but no bass. However, it wasn't a dance track; it was the rap equivalent of a ballad, pushed up by female backing vocals and a sample of bubbling liquid.

Having sucked in the audience, OutKast was taking them on a mind trip—only the mind trip was through *their* minds. If they hadn't been so good, taking the ride with them might have been impossible. It was tough enough for some folks. But they were doing it with such confidence and certainty that it was impossible not to listen and be impressed by the things they were saying.

It made sense to close with a track that was more up. And that was a slower remix of "Elevators (Me & You)" that changed the feel to straight hip-hop at eighty-six beats per minute and pushed the voices right up front. It was a relief after the intensity of the last few tracks, which had been more like a suite.

It was ahead of its time by throwing off all the conventions of hip-hop and going exactly where Dre and Big Boi wanted to go. It was conscious, aware of America's social problems, in the black community and in the country as a whole. And it certainly wasn't afraid to talk about real life—the bad as well as the good.

Though they were listening to more and more music, it was still soul that was the overwhelming vibe of the music. And that suited what they were saying. The best soul singers—Marvin Gaye, Stevie Wonder, Curtis Mayfield, and others—had all looked outside for inspiration. With so much hip-hop stuck in a musical loop, what *ATL*iens offered up was refreshing. More than that, it was necessary.

It was also remarkable that the album sold as well as it did. But OutKast had strong commercial instincts to complement their art. The video for "ATLiens," for example, began in a very Afrocentric way (in addition to showing Dre and Big Boi as freedom fighters), exploring a pyramid—whose tunnels led to a club. It was the very best of both worlds.

Their big hope was that hip-hop would follow their lead and become more creative. If they could sell albums that way, then other acts could, too. This school of thought demanded as much imagination and skill on the part of others, though, and it quickly became obvious that was lacking. OutKast were a one-off.

Onstage OutKast was going to push it, too. Dre and Big Boi had a tour lined up with Goodie MOb, fellow Atlanteans, and the young men promised something startling. That was what OutKast promised and provided: a set full of funk and science fiction, with a stage straight out of the mothership.

The young men had every reason to be proud of what they'd done. The first album, as Dre explained, "was just a go-for-what-you-know-like-a-wild-thing, 'this is our first chance, we're just going to do it.'" Which was fine, but ultimately it wasn't satisfying artistically, so "the second album was definitely more serious and more thought-provoking, like for cooling out and thinking."

There was also some anger behind it, much of it at the music business, which, they felt, used black kids, making money off their rapping, then throwing them aside.

"We feel it's mostly black kids getting shafted," said Dre. "We were like that at first. We didn't know the business side of things. We just wanted to make music that means something to us, get onstage and rock the crowd."

They remained, firmly and very proudly, outsiders.

"We're still ATLiens," Dre agreed. "The ATL for Atlanta, and the aliens for our status in the hip-hop game."

The studio experience they'd gained showed in the fact that this time around they produced some of the tracks themselves, instead of relying completely on Organized Noize. "ATLiens,"

"Wheelz of Steel," "Elevators (Me & You)," "Ova Da Wudz," and "E.T. (Extraterrestrial)" were all done by the pair, and they were all cuts that worked outside conventional hip-hop. They'd gained a deeper understanding and appreciation of the recording process, just as they were gaining a deeper understanding of themselves. There was no standing still with OutKast.

"We don't let anyone tell us how we're going to make it, though," Big Boi said about the music. "If it's dope and it's got a feel to it, we'll do it. We don't set up no boundaries."

For Andre, that meant no boundaries in clothing. As he explained it, he'd simply become bored with the way everyone was dressing.

"I bought this turban and started to wear it. Thought it looked cool. I started buying one-of-a-kind things from thrift stores . . . I had girls who were making things for me, these outfits I drew." But coloring outside the lines meant being misunderstood. "I don't think the hip-hop community had ever seen anything like it before. They didn't understand what the fuck was going on. The record company would say to Big Boi, 'Hey, talk to him.' He'd tell me the shit they were saying, but at the same time, it was new to him." New and confusing. He'd accept it in his partner, although he really didn't have a clue what to do about it, or how to present himself, other than as himself. It caused disagreements between the two of them, which sparked more rumors of a breakup. But they'd been together too long and become too close to let something like clothes come between them. Style had always been an important factor for them both, and if Dre's style was getting strange, well, Antwan didn't have to follow, only accept, and go his own sartorial way—which he did.

However, there was also another story behind the turban, one that tied into some of the music they were making on the album. To chill after the first disc, Andre took a vacation in Jamaica, the home of reggae, and was impressed by the dreadlocks worn by the Rastafarians there. (The Rastas are a sect that believes in the holiness of the late Emperor Haile Selassie of Ethiopia and that the spiritual home of black people is in Ethiopia. The Rastas are also vegetarians and teetotalers; their sacrament is marijuana. Plenty of major roots reggae figures, including Bob Marley, have adopted the Rasta lifestyle and spirit.) Andre liked the dreadlocks so much that he began to grow his own. At home, though, he wanted to keep them wrapped. Instead of opting for the tam worn by so many Rastas, he wanted something more individual, so he began to wear a turban. The Jamaican vacation would explain the fact that ideas from reggae and dub could be heard on *ATLiens*.

Preparing for the tour, then actually being out on the road, took up plenty of 1997. By now Dre and Big Boi were big stars, but that didn't stop them taking the tour bus, rather than living the high life. They were smart enough to know that a little economy pays off in the long run.

And when they weren't working, Big Boi had his pit bull kennel going, where he was always happy to spend time, especially since it was right by his house—where he'd notoriously had a stripper's pole installed in the basement.

Dre had also developed a life outside music. He'd begun painting and selling the canvases he finished (like the kennel, there's an ad for his paintings in the CD booklet of *Speakerboxxx/The Love Below*). It was another outlet for his creativity, this time visually, rather than with words or sound.

He also met a rising star, with whom he'd become very close. To hear Dre rap about it later, he first noticed Erykah Badu because she wore a turban like his. But her head wrap was a gesture to Africa, and her name was solely for herself. Born Erica Wright in Dallas, Texas, she'd first performed with her mother, Kolleen, a professional actress, when she was four. The oldest of three children, she'd changed her "slave name" as a teenager to Erykah Badu, with the "kah" in Erykah coming from a word for inner self, while "Badu" was for the jazz scat singers.

Like Dre, she didn't live her personal life in the mainstream.

"I am a nonconformist," she declared. "All of my life I have been slightly to the left, a little different."

She'd first been noticed in 1994 by singer D'Angelo and had recorded with him, although it was 1997 when her first album, *Baduizm*, hit the stores, and the single "On and On" cruised to number two with its languid, soulful groove under her remarkable, individual voice. She stood out in fashion and music, so it was no surprise that Dre was attracted. And it made sense that she'd click right back.

On both sides it was love, a very deep and real love that went beyond the physical to the spiritual. While they didn't marry, they were as close as many married couples. Neither of them took the idea of family and real relationships lightly, since they were very close to their own families and understood just what those bonds meant. So the idea of having a child was something to be discussed. It was a huge commitment on both sides, but one they both wanted.

So when Erykah realized she was pregnant, it was a major step for them both, one that involved a lot of planning and a lot of discussions, especially as she was just coming into her own with the success of her album. Being who she was, though, life was more important to her than her career, but she just could not ignore the momentum of the single and the quality of the album she'd made. She tried to tour, early in the pregnancy, with Wu-Tang Clan, but life on the road and carrying a child didn't mix well.

The child of Dre and Erykah, Seven Sirius (The name Seven, Badu explained, was because "it's a divine number that can't be divided"), was born at Badu's home in Dallas on November 18, 1996, with the assistance of a midwife.

It was actually a double birth. The same day that Seven arrived, so did her second album, *Erykah Badu Live*. Of course, the baby was far more important, and she'd already decided to take time off to raise him. But Dre was an important part of the parenting process, too. Seven was his child as much as hers, and they were a couple, dedicated not only to each other, but to bringing their son up right.

As much as anything, that involved time. Babies do sleep a lot, but when they're awake, they demand attention—and parents are usually happy to lavish it on them. But for someone like Andre, whose work didn't adhere to a regular schedule and whose business was in another city—Atlanta—that was both difficult and easy. Difficult because work was starting on the next OutKast album, and easy because, when he wasn't working, he could devote all his time to his family. There were times he'd be gone for extended periods and other times when he would spend weeks at home.

But even when Dre was at home, that didn't mean all the music vanished from his mind—or from Erykah's. One of the biggest surprises was that they never recorded any straight duets together (although Badu guested on two OutKast albums). Nor has anything they might have written together been released.

Working as part of a band meant collaborating a lot. Dre couldn't simply lock himself away in the studio alone. He had to be communicating with Big Boi. And though their ideas were taking separate paths, they were still very much a band.

The responsibility of fatherhood inevitably wrought changes on Dre. It made him more aware of his place in the world—and his own duties. It also brought home how important relationships are—things that happen to most new parents.

Undoubtedly Dre and Erykah introduced each other to their musical loves, too. In Erykah's case, her two great inspirations were Nina Simone and Billie Holiday. For Dre, of course, anything could be an inspiration, whether it was Led Zeppelin playing "Kashmir" or Curtis Mayfield on "Freddie's Dead." The young couple shared a leaning toward spirituality that helped keep them close and on the right path. That didn't mean renouncing worldly goods and living ascetic lives. They could still enjoy the comforts they'd earned through their art. It meant living responsibly and being willing to be responsible for their own lives—and that of their son.

Dre had given up weed and alcohol a couple of years before; he felt that they clouded the mind, rather than opening it. He was living life his own way, on his own terms. And the more he discovered about himself, the more individual his music would become.

On *ATLiens* OutKast had taken a giant step. But the simple truth was that it was just another small step. Having started down that path, there could be no turning back. They hadn't managed to confound fans with *ATLiens*; instead, more fans than ever had accepted them, which was like a license to go wherever they wanted.

Ideas could come from anywhere: a word, a beat, a conversation, something seen; it all became fodder for the imagination.

"Anything in the world can spark up a song and when you

get in the studio you can have an idea for a lyric and then you put music behind it or vice versa," Dre said. So much of it came from the vibe, rather than a specific idea. Music is created from the moment, even if the studio performances can take weeks or even months sometimes.

By understanding where they were going, Dre and Big Boi could control it—at least, if they wanted to. They'd learned from what they'd done in the past, and they could use those experiences for the future.

While OutKast existed as a group, the young men were also part of a greater whole: the Dungeon collective that had come together around Organized Noize. In addition to OutKast, Goodie MOb and Cool Breeze all helped each other out in the studio. (Members of Goodie MOb had been on both of Out-Kast's albums, for instance.)

While things did seem quiet in the OutKast camp, they did keep things spinning. Not only did "ATLiens" and "Jazzy Belle" get plenty of airplay—the former even had a video—but they also contributed a song, "In Due Time," to the soundtrack of the movie *Soul Food*. It helped keep their name and profile in front of people.

That was probably more of a business decision than an artistic one, but it remained important. The time when it was just possible to release a single or an album and let the music speak for itself had long since passed. Now so many things had to be orchestrated. The marketing of an act and a CD was an art in itself—not that OutKast ever made that too easy.

4. AQUEMINI

"WHEN WE started doing the more experimental rap, started talking about aliens, that's when more and more white people started coming to the shows," noted Dre. "We're from the 'hood, but that's not where our music stayed."

That was an important point. They'd done what very few hip-hop acts had managed; they'd crossed over to that bigger suburban audience. Kids who were mostly into alternative music were even willing to listen to them, because of what was going on musically on *ATLiens*. For them, it wasn't about the beats or the fact that OutKast had enjoyed some hits. It was the grab bag in the contents that appealed.

It was about keeping an open mind, something that was, well, alien to a lot of people in hip-hop.

"I've met a lot of producers who know exactly what they're looking for. It's like etched in stone before they begin. But we start with one element and build on it until we get to a point where we say, 'Yeah, that's it. That's jammin'.'"

OutKast was beginning to gain respect. Not only in hip-hop, where they were still looked at a bit strangely, but in rock music, too—they could talk as knowledgeably about their rock influences as they could about anything from soul to reggae to old school hip-hop. They could cite anything from Bob Marley to N.W.A., from R.E.M. to the heavy metal band AC/DC, and even Big Boi's early favorite: the eccentric Kate Bush.

The fact that *both* Dre and Big Boi perused the whole range of music gave them a huge palette of ideas to work from, which was more than evident on *Aquemini*, which arrived in September 1998.

Aquemini hadn't taken any longer to make than their last album, but it generated a renewed sense of purpose, making the two previous efforts seem like warm-up exercises, as if they'd simply been flexing their muscles. There were plenty of guests, including Goodie MOb members, of course, and Raekwon, but also George Clinton, the godfather of space funk, who'd been such an inspiration for *ATLiens*.

They'd been serious about their music before, of course, but this time out they were determined to nail it: to grab the funk of their debut and many of the lyrical concerns of the second disc and serve them up together, but refined and even funkier—and further out there, yet in a way that made sense. There'd always been an internal logic to their weirdness. Now they were good enough to make strange seem fully commercial.

Just where they were coming from was apparent from the first single, the stinging "Rosa Parks." The track took its name from one of the icons of the 1950s. On December 1, 1955, at the age of forty-two, tired from a long day at work in Montgomery, Alabama, Rosa Parks refused to give up her seat in the front of the bus to a white man. Her refusal to move to the back of the bus, remaining up front in an area reserved for whites during those days of segregation, became a landmark event in American history. From that small action the spark of the civil rights movement was fanned into a flame (actually, she was the third black person to refuse to move, but it was her cause that was taken up by the NAACP). Parks was arrested and challenged the constitutionality of Alabama's segregation laws. On the day of her trial, blacks boycotted Montgomery's bus system. Parks was convicted, as was expected. In the wake of that court decision, the Montgomery Improvement Association was formed, headed up by a young minister, Dr. Martin Luther King, Jr. It took a year to desegregate the city's bus system, but the wheels had slowly begun to roll toward the full integration of blacks in America.

"Rosa Parks" actually had very little to do with the real person—her name wasn't even mentioned in the song. The closest it came was mentioning "back of the bus," and that in the same breath as "crunk," the slang name for the Southern booty-shaking bass style. But it had a magnificent chorus that it was impossible not to sing along with. There was a veiled reference to Erykah Badu, the "Gypsy," but beyond that it was representing OutKast, Atlanta, and the South (especially in the pronunciation of "fuss," which was almost impossible to make out without the lyrics in the booklet). What made the track, though, outside its chorus over some acoustic guitar chords, was the harmonica breakdown in the middle. That couldn't have come from anywhere but the South, where the harmonica and black music had been linked for decades, most particularly in blues. It was daring in its regression. The harmonica was virtually a symbol of the rural South, the Mississippi Delta, and country blues (although it had also played an important part in the urban blues of Chicago). It looked back to the time of prejudice, which made its inclusion symbolic and ironic, especially in what was really a party anthem.

This was hip-hop, but it was a lot more. The rhythm was rock, the references were blues and even gospel in the harmonies, and it built around a number of elements, including a vocal line that was almost scatted. The video for the track took that and ran with it, especially in its presentation of Andre, wearing furry, multicolored pants and football pads. There was a marching band dancing in the street (some of the dance moves slyly referenced M.C. Hammer and his moves for "U Can't Touch This," a big hit of the early '90s that sampled Rick James's "Superfreak," one of the very first tracks to really cross over from funk to rock). It was a piece of joy. But really, it had very little, if anything, to do with Rosa Parks.

Rosa Parks herself noticed that when it was brought to her attention. Certainly it was true that OutKast was using her name without permission. But it was also a fact that her name was widely known and taught in schools all over America and the world. However, since there was nothing about her in the song, it could have been seen as an attempt to cash in on her celebrity, virtually false advertising. The song also contained some profanity, which didn't sit well with the modest Ms. Parks, making it, in her mind, a commercial misappropriation of her name and a taint on her place in history.

She sued OutKast—and LaFace—on those grounds. In return, the band and their label argued that, since Parks was a public figure, the First Amendment guaranteed free speech and allowed the use of her name. It was an unfortunate battle. Out-Kast had intended the use of the name Rosa Parks as a tribute to a great woman, not as anything derogatory (she'd also been the subject of at least one previous song, the Neville Brothers' "Sister Rosa"). But to line up against such a revered person in court certainly wasn't good. The suit first entered court in Michigan in November 1999, although Parks had first lodged a formal complaint in March, and negotiations had begun then.

"[OutKast] did not confer with Mrs. Parks about using her name or likeness in the song in question," Parks's representative said, "and she views this as the same kind of conduct that she faced forty years ago, an abuse of people."

Seeking to come to an agreement, at the time of the complaint OutKast had said: "Rosa Parks has inspired our music and our lives since we were children. The opportunity to use our music to help educate young people about the heroes in the African-American community is one of the responsibilities we feel we have as music artists. It was not, nor ever has been our intention to defame a woman who we consider a role model and a civil rights pioneer. We hope to be able to work out this situation amicably."

And LaFace was also dismayed by the situation.

"Both the label and OutKast have enormous respect for Ms. Parks and the accomplishments and contributions she has made to the Civil Rights movement," wrote LaFace General Manager Dorsey James. "We are actively working to inform Ms. Parks's representatives of our deep dismay concerning this situation and bring it to an expeditious and amicable close."

Unfortunately, it had been impossible to reach a settlement of any kind, so the battle lines were drawn in Michigan. And there

Parks lost, as the Federal Court sided with the band and the label.

However, that was far from the end of the story. Parks and her attorneys filed an appeal, which was heard in early 2003 by a three-judge panel of the 6th U.S. Circuit Court of Appeals in Cincinnati, Ohio. They found in favor of Parks, at least to the extent of reinstating part of her lawsuit.

From there it became even messier. OutKast and LaFace appealed to the Supreme Court, the ultimate legal authority in the country, to have the case thrown out. But in December 2003, after the single had long since come and gone, the Court refused to intervene in the case. That action, taken without any comment from the Justices, meant that Parks, who was then ninety, could go ahead with her lawsuit.

Later in the month it was reported that the two parties were finally close to reaching an out-of-court settlement on the matter. According to one source, Arista Records (the ultimate party responsible, as owner of LaFace) agreed to produce CDs and DVDs to educate people about Parks and the civil rights struggle in Alabama. The label had tried for a settlement involving a benefit concert, the proceeds of which would go to charity, but Parks and her attorneys had said no. The financial part of the settlement had still to be agreed upon.

Obviously, neither Dre nor Big Boi had anticipated all that would follow when they named the song. It's a reasonable assumption, from their natures, that they had nothing but admiration for the woman and had absolutely no intention of making it seem as if the song was ridiculing or defaming her. And probably the very last thing they wanted was a confrontation with her, either inside court or out. It certainly wasn't a publicity stunt of any kind; all the publicity they'd receive from it would be negative, given Parks's stature—and it wasn't as if they needed extra press, anyway. They were already a major force in hip-hop.

All in all, it was unfortunate. But what was done, was done, and there could be no turning back from it. They'd been contrite in their statement prior to the first court appearance. However, Parks's stance was understandable. Her unblemished reputation was what she had, and it was only natural she'd want to keep it that way.

About the only positive thing for OutKast was that the legal fuss didn't blow up until the song and album were essentially a part of their past, rather than when it was actually happening. That didn't exactly make things any better, but it perhaps limited some of the damage and fallout among African-Americans that accrued from the situation.

At the time of its release, though, probably few who heard the song actively associated it with Ms. Parks in a negative way. Her very name and the mention of "back of the bus" triggered its own image of civil rights, and beyond that the song was taken on its own terms—as the band had probably intended.

All those legal difficulties were in the future, however. For now there was a record made, and it needed promoting. *Aquemini*, named for the combined birth signs of Big Boi (Aquarius) and Dre (Gemini), was the first real knockout punch from Out-Kast. In *Aquemini* they refined the funk of the first album, filtering it through all the listening they'd done since, and added the lyrical consciousness of *ATLiens*, but in a much more easily digestible fashion.

One of the more interesting points was that they were responsible for most of the production on this album. They were still very much a part of the Dungeon family (as the tattoos on

Big Boi's forearms showed), but they'd grown and learned. They knew their way around a studio now and had the tools do develop their ideas fully. Seven of the album's sixteen cuts were OutKast productions, and they demonstrated the fact that Andre and Antwan had come fully into their own. They now had the power to transform their visions into reality. They'd even begun their own production company, Earthtone III, to handle these productions and work they intended to do with other artists.

In fact, one of those other artists contributed to *Aquemini*. David "Mr. DJ" Sheats handled production chores on three of the album's cuts, showing himself to be a very strong beatmaster and arranger. Erykah Badu also made an appearance, not only cowriting but adding her very distinctive voice to "Liberation."

It was an album of epic scope, but after two outings OutKast was finally ready to make that leap. Just how epic became obvious as "Return of the 'G'" unfolded, adding strings to its stripped-down bass and drums. It was a nod to the gangsta rap that was so popular, but also a refutation of it, an alternative in the rhymes and the lives that were happening for most people. It tried to show that there was another way than being a thug—which had become a fashion statement as much as a ghetto lifestyle.

"Everybody want to be a thug, man," Dre told *Source*. "[But] people are just scared to [be original]. But everybody waiting on that nigga to do it . . . So you have to be a strong nigga to take that ridicule."

Dre and Big Boi were both strong. And they were just getting stronger. The critics were right behind them when they heard it. *Source* magazine, in a rare move that had happened barely a handful of times in the publication's existence, awarded the record a complete five mics—their highest rating.

Although Dre initially said that the review and rating was "a real blessing" that "was really helpful," Big Boi would dismiss all that in a later interview.

"Hell, fuck that. What it really means is that it means something to the people who read *The Source*, which is supposed to be hip-hop's bible. At first, you're probably like, well . . . I mean you see the ratings they give to different albums, and you probably be like 'Damn, how did they get this, and how did he get that?' So what it is, it's . . . politics. So that whole rating system of *The Source* don't mean shit to us."

For all his objections, it probably helped them a great deal. But there was more than one magazine raving about the disc: *Entertainment Weekly*, which reached a much broader audience, called it the "hip-hop album of the year," which was no small tag.

More than anything, in spite of limited airplay of the "Rosa Parks" video, they were reaching a lot of people. The album hit stores in September 1998; two months later it had already sold a million copies, easily outstripping their previous album in terms of speed. It also brought them recognition from the recording establishment when "Rosa Parks" was nominated for a Grammy for Best Rap Performance by a Duo or Group. While they didn't win, it meant they were very firmly on the map and deep into the mainstream. The fact that *Aquemini* would go on to sell over two million copies was proof that they arrived in the big time and that hip-hop had room for art inside its expanding boundaries.

To be fair, a lot of those sales didn't come from the hard-core hip-hop heads, but from the suburbs. OutKast had really and completely crossed over to become a hip-hop band that rock fans actively sought out, simply because there was something new going on in the music, and it was a sound rock fans could understand and relate to, while still being authentic hip-hop.

It was also an adventure. Dre characterized the album as the place where they "just started to put our feet into cold water. We just started to get a little bit free with it. So it became more of a soulful album; it was what we believed in."

At the same time, Big Boi and Dre understood this was just one more step on the journey. They could be pleased and proud of what they'd done, but it still wasn't the best that they could do. As artists, they were constantly dissatisfied, and continual questing came with the territory, especially if you were injecting some spirituality into the mix, and OutKast was definitely doing that.

Their world had grown huge. They'd gone from East Point and College Park to take Atlanta, the United States, and even other parts of the world, as they'd already toured Europe. Certainly their next tour was going to be interesting, a trip around the United States opening for Lauryn Hill, the very conscious singer and rapper from the Fugees, the band that had broken wide open with their version of "Killing Me Softly with His Song" and their album *The Score* in 1996. Now she was touring on the back of her very adventurous solo disc, *The Miseducation of Lauryn Hill*, which had come out in 1998.

It was a great pairing. Hill's roots were in hip-hop, but she'd extended them into so much more, and the messages in her music were positive but real. In other words, the two acts complemented each other perfectly. It was a double bill that could cross all kinds of barriers.

One track on *Aquemini* reportedly had its roots in sessions that had happened long before the album was recorded. "West Savannah," according to some, originally dated from the first album, *Southernplayalisticadillacmuzik*, although it never appeared on that record. It was very much Antwan's track, recorded with Organized Noize (Dre doesn't even appear in the credits), a tale that could easily have been his autobiography—but wasn't. But the fact that it was without Dre doesn't really make it the precursor of his *Speakerboxxx* solo disc at all; there'd be a long road to travel before then. The biggest question is: Why was it included now? A couple of possible reasons stand out.

The first is simply because it's that good and needed to be on a record, but this was the first where it could really fit lyrically. The second is that they knew it was a good track and wanted to use it to fill out *Aquemini* to its fullest possible length. (It runs just a few seconds short of seventy-five minutes.)

It was straight Southern soul, with horns, a sweet guitar line, and an organ underneath that was straight out of church. Musically it could have come from Stax or Muscle Shoals, which was a stark contrast to the gangsta content of the lyrics. There was irony in there, but also a straightforward portrayal of real life for some people without any praise for the violence that went with the lifestyle—merely a subtle point that it was all a dead end.

It was that rarest of albums in any genre—one without a single weak track. And at the same time, the quality was so high that there wasn't a single cut that stood above the rest, with everything so good. If there was one song that came close to not cutting it, it was "Mamacita," but even that redeemed itself.

By using three producers (themselves, Organized Noize, and David Sheats) OutKast mixed up the sound. Sheats brought a very original ethic, best heard on both parts of "Da Art of Story-tellin'," especially the second part, where the sense of urgency and doom was almost palpable.

Dre and Big Boi's own ideas were also startling—and never

more so than on "Synthesizer." Bringing George Clinton in as a guest was almost a no-brainer; in many ways—he was the godfather of what OutKast was doing. And the subject matter of the track—about the way technology was making society and life less real—dovetailed with a lot of what Clinton had been saying. Finishing with a capella vocals—Dre and Big Boi showing surprisingly good singing voices—the cut traveled from the future to the past musically, a remarkably well-thought-out piece of music. A lot of work went into the arrangement, and it showed—but seamlessly.

Every piece of *Aquemini* fitted together to paint an unflinching picture not only of African-American society, but of America as a whole. It stood as the most serious album to have come out of hip-hop, and one that offered a way forward lyrically—such as in the message of redemption that ended "Slump" (and turned into the crying of a baby—the future—over a soulful little groove).

It had almost become a trademark for OutKast to have plenty of guitar on their albums, and it was all over "Spottieottiedopalicious." More than anything they'd done before, it was their homage to the great Curtis Mayfield, who used the falsetto vocals that were also the chorus here. The horns offered a nod to reggae in their slight wonkiness, as did the touches of dub effects toward the end of the track. OutKast knew their music and used it judiciously to serve the song. But again, it was the subject matter that really caught the ear. There was no machismo or posturing, just slices of real life—real life in the ghetto. And it wasn't glamorous.

"Y' All Sacred" ratcheted up the exposure of feelings. It wasn't part of hip-hop, with its very masculine attitude, to admit fear of anything, but this song did. Being willing to expose themselves that way, to even point out that fear was an option, showed a new sensitivity in OutKast's lyrics. The track built slowly, with layers of tension folding over each other as the rhymes spit out over a loop. In a way, by being willing to expose emotions, the song was the forerunner of their huge hit "Ms. Jackson."

None of the songs watched their language; OutKast never had (which was why all their albums had parental advisory stickers). But it would have been wrong to have moderated the speech; it simply wouldn't have reflected their own reality.

One facet of what was becoming the genius of OutKast was the way they sequenced *Aquemini*. "Y'All Scared" was followed by the chilled-out consciousness of "Liberation," which took a different, jazzier groove (possibly influenced by Erykah Badu, who was on the cut). The spirit of Gil Scott-Heron was all over it. His songs of the '70s had projected a black consciousness, mixing it with jazz and finding a white audience.

For all that "Liberation" seemed somewhat formless, it was a fabulous jam—and one that didn't use samples or beats, but all live instruments, taking the music in yet another direction. Even Big Boi's rapping was more poetry than anything. (At its best, rap *is* poetry.)

What impressed more than anything was the breadth of vision on the record. It literally expanded the definition of hip-hop into so many areas. For the first time, OutKast was being referred to as the Beatles of the genre, and it was a good analogy. Throughout the decade of the '60s the Beatles had constantly pushed at the boundaries of pop music in an attempt to heighten people's awareness of music as an art form. As a result, pop music started to be taken more seriously. The Beatles brought in ideas and elements that no one had considered before and helped make them part of the standard lexicon of the music. Even today bands are still imitating them.

OutKast's achievement on *Aquemini* was almost the equivalent of the Beatles's positive psychedelic trail blazing on *Revolver*. As if to echo that experimental era, OutKast finished the album with "Chonkyfire," in which the musical elements came exclusively from rock 'n' roll (which was even mentioned in the chorus), filtered through the black rock consciousness of bands like Living Color. It messed with the head, which was the point.

It had taken OutKast a pair of albums to really come up to speed, but now they were cruising, and their Cadillac had overtaken all the Benzes and Lexuses. Sometimes the true groundbreakers never get acknowledged until years later; but sometimes they manage to attain respect immediately, and that was what was happening to OutKast; all the plaudits for *Aquemini* were completely deserved.

They'd taken hip-hop to the next level, pushing it further than ever before. The fact that they'd been so successful by taking extreme chances showed the way for others to follow—and in time maybe even pass them. But that was the nature of music. Someone had to lead the way.

They were two very different people with one tight bond holding them together. As Big Boi listed it, "I smoke. He don't smoke. I go to strip clubs. He don't go to strip clubs. He used to, you know what I'm saying? I mean, that individualism. And that's what OutKast is all about."

Big Boi was more firmly wedded to hip-hop than Dre, and that was fine. Dre might be straining at the leash, but he wasn't completely off it yet. They were both exploring; it was just that sometimes Dre went a bit further, in his dress as well as his ideas.

"To funk it up and start wearing elaborate clothing is all a part of the music to me. I'm always trying to find new ways to keep myself excited."

In other words, he needed his look to reflect his sound, for it to be every bit as funky as the music he made, and he was obviously hitting on all levels, to judge by some of the outfits he sported, including a platinum blond wig.

For the vast majority of fans, however, the bottom line was all about the music, and whether that satisfied, which it very obviously did. By July of 1999 they'd sold two million copies of *Aquemini*, and music magazine *Spin* had it listed at number thirty-five in its ninety greatest albums of the '90s. That was not only a measure of its critical acclaim, but also of its commercial success.

The 1999 tour went well, and after that they should have taken more time off. They did manage a little space, as Big Boi chilled with his dogs in Fayetteville and hung in Atlanta, while Dre shuttled back and forth between home and Dallas, spending time with Erykah and their son. He was happy to give Seven plenty of attention, doing all the things a father should do and being a good example of a parent.

There was still plenty of business happening, though. The pair guested on the "Watch for the Hook" single by fellow Dungeon family members Cool Breeze, which topped the rap singles charts for three weeks. Big Boi was everywhere, appearing with the lauded Missy Elliott on her "All N My Grill" and along with the Youngbloodz on "85." Notably both were Southern projects, with Elliott from Virginia and the Youngbloodz Atlanta homeboys.

The time was also right for Dre and Big Boi to start their own label, Aquemini, named for their album. For some artists, having a label could be pure vanity, an illustration of the power they wielded within the business. But OutKast was serious about it. They planned on developing underground Atlanta talent and providing an outlet for new voices to be heard. They'd even made their first signing, a local rapper named Slimm Calhoun, who was a part of the extended Dungeon family. And more would come, too, like Backbone, whose tales of thug life finally appeared on *Concrete Law* in 2001, a year after Calhoun's debut, *The Skinny*. In fact, OutKast would take Calhoun on tour with them in 2000 to perform some of the tracks from his album. And there would also be Killer Mike . . . but his work with them was still around the corner.

Because of the very nature of things, the day-to-day running of the label was left up to others. But the decisions all came from Big Boi and Dre. They'd been involved in music long enough to have a solid understanding of how the business worked. They wanted to promote new talent, but Dre and Big Boi were understandably selective. And although their own musical tastes were all over the place, the artists they signed would all be connected with hip-hop, since that remained the root that they understood best of all.

As Earthtone III they also planned on being more involved in various production projects, too. It was obvious from *Aquemini* that they both had developed a good feel for the studio and real flair for beats, samples, and instruments. While their focus would always be OutKast, of course, that wouldn't stop them from looking elsewhere as producers if the opportunity should arise.

The bottom line, though, was artistry. Anyone and everyone

could release hip-hop CDs (and sometimes it seemed that everyone did), but OutKast was beginning to move on from hip-hop, to build new bridges to vistas beyond. That said, *Aquemini* remained very much a recognizable hip-hop disc— and proud of it.

There was no standing still for OutKast. By now it should have been clear that when they returned there'd be no rehashing of the past. They'd build on what they achieved and take it further; that was their nature. It was also their power. If other rappers wanted to stay still, they could, but they'd end up the losers artistically, even if they bought the jewelry and the cars. Dre and Big Boi were smarter than that. They could afford the luxuries, but they were also investing a lot of the money they made, laying the groundwork for life in the future.

Hip-hop was still a young enough form that it was impossible to make predictions about long careers. Would older rappers still be viable artistically or would hip-hop stay a form for the young? A couple of decades before, the thought of rock bands still touring in their sixties had seemed ridiculous, but it was happening now, and they (the Rolling Stones, in particular) were pulling in huge grosses. There was still a market for the music they made. Would the same thing happen with hip-hop? Honestly, no one knew. At least by investing their earnings, Dre and Big Boi would never go hungry if it did all fall apart.

And sometimes in life, things did just fall apart.

The hardest part of life can be when romances simply don't work out. Sometimes just admitting it's not working takes a big leap of faith. But by the beginning of 2000 it was obvious to Dre and Erykah that whatever they'd had no longer existed. The problem there was that they also had a son, which always complicates matters.

In some ways, they were in a luckier position than most couples; they had money, which can soften any blow. But breaking the news of their split to their son wouldn't be easy.

They'd always kept their relationship very private and out of the public eye; but neither of them had ever sought celebrity status. They made music, and that was the vocation for both of them in life. And they both were mature enough to understand all the implications of ending a relationship. They would remain tied for life through their son; both of them were completely committed to giving him a good upbringing.

That didn't mean there was no pain in the split; there was plenty of that. As Erykah put it, "We are not a functioning couple, but we are a family. So therefore, I am not a single mother. My son has both a father and a mother who are very responsible."

After three years together, it was over. Badu wrote about it on her album, *Mama's Gun*, in the ten-minute track "Green Eyes." Dre had actively encouraged her to do so, to explore her feelings and get them out in the way she knew best—and also to show other people that they shouldn't beat themselves up over breakups.

Dre would be, and still is, a very active father. That was his promise, and he has stuck to it. They both put their son first, more than many other couples; Seven hasn't been caught in any crossfire. Instead they've behaved with a remarkable dignity throughout the transition.

It would also prove that Erykah wasn't the only one to put her feelings about the breakup to music. Dre was going to do that on their next album. For that one, though, there was going to be more branching out.

A band that experiments needs a place to try things out. The one piece of the puzzle really missing from the OutKast empire was that space. Now they were ready to make the move to own their own recording studio, which they would call Stankonia Studios. The place they bought was previously known as Bosstown Studios (they'd worked there on their first and second albums, in fact), which had been owned by Bobby Brown, the singer who'd become better known for his busts and his marriage to Whitney Houston than for any of his music in recent years. OutKast bought Bosstown studios in 1999 and refurbished it with the state-of-the-art equipment they needed for their own work. Apart from the control room, there was also a small live room, able to accommodate several musicians at once, albeit in rather cramped conditions, but other vocals rooms existed as well.

With such a facility, they could take their time and spend as many hours trying things as they desired. That was important. Buying studio time wasn't cheap, and the whole technology of recording was constantly evolving, with analogue tape now a thing of the past, replaced by digital formats like Pro Tools, which offered a lot more options in smaller packages.

The fact that OutKast kept pushing forward necessarily meant a lot of time in the studio—although maybe not quite as much as some people imagined. Both Dre and Big Boi had studios at home, smaller ones where they could work, putting down basic ideas and developing them a little. Work on the next album actually began on December 1, 1999, although the record was promised quickly. That was unlikely, though. Big Boi and Dre continued to spread their wings: Organized Noize would handle production on just a couple of tracks and one track would have Carl Mo behind the control board; OutKast would produce all the other tracks. Satisfying as that was, it more than doubled the work.

The big question was: How could they progress after *Aquemini*? That was the challenge they set themselves, but it was one they both loved. They were constantly changing, and the new record could only reflect where they were when they were doing it. These days Dre was looking like nobody so much as Jimi Hendrix, the outstanding guitarist who revolutionized the instrument in the late '60s, before choking to death after taking barbituates in 1970. Bandanas around a spreading bushy Afro, a goatee, and psychedelic colors in his clothes were the order of the day. No more baggy jeans; it was tight leather pants now, looking more like a rock star than anyone involved in hip-hop. Even Big Boi had grown his hair out and grown a goatee. He could still look sharp, but he was favoring a more casual look.

Big things were in the air when they finally hit the studio. Some ideas were in place, but plenty more were cooked up as they worked, one thing sparking another, as had always been the case. In the world of music, as they'd learned, anything was possible; they only had to use their imaginations. And neither of them was lacking in that department.

5. STANKONIA

FOR MOST artists, the act of creating a new album would take up all of their time. It definitely was the focus for OutKast. But they also needed other outlets, places where they could show their vision. Dre had his painting, and Big Boi, of course, had his dogs. But there are other ways to make your mark in the world.

Having their own clothing line was a completely natural extension for OutKast. From the time Big Boi and Dre met they'd been about style almost as much as music. Those styles might have diverged, but they were still an integral part of who both band members were. And these days, with so many rappers launching their own clothing lines, like ROCAWEAR or Sean

John, there was nothing outrageous or even odd about getting into the rag trade. It would only start getting tricky if they began making reproductions of Dre's wardrobe. *That* would probably be going a bit too far for most people. What they envisioned, Dre said, slightly tongue in cheek, was something for "men, children, women, and, of course, your dogs; so you'll be able to get something for everybody."

While the first lines didn't appear until the spring of 2001, the nature of the clothing business was such that they had to plan a full year ahead. The big department stores like Macy's and Bloomingdale's agreed to carry the line, and plenty of other urban stores also lined up for the opportunity.

The designs—at least the conception and sketches—came directly from OutKast. This line was more than a name; it was a reflection of their ideas and tastes.

OutKast Clothing Company was about the "fresh and clean" ethos that comprised part of OutKast's image—so much so that it became the title of a song from the new album. Initially they tested the waters with simple items, everyday clothing like T-shirts and jeans, before venturing deeper into fashion. It made sense. When the basic items sold well, the company would expand.

It turned out that OutKast had a magic touch in clothing stores as well as on the charts. The first year saw new investors and the line expanded to include boys' clothing. By the end of 2003, womens' and girls' ranges were also available in stores.

Unlike the brands of other rappers and producers, which gained their cachet by being hip-hop clothing, OutKast looked outside those boundaries (given their history, anything less would have been surprising). The baggy silhouettes of hip-hop gear were now only one facet as the company moved into more contemporary sportswear, even into the higher range of outerwear, which includes leather jackets.

How successful was it? Well, it didn't pose a challenge to the major designer labels, but by the end of 2002 they were doing well enough to add a line for discount stores. Rather than the normal winged OutKast logo that was their trademark (the wings, incidentally, are a reference to how fly they are), the discount line simply had the word OutKast on the clothes.

Whichever way they turned, OutKast had the Midas touch.

Clothing was fun, something to be enjoyed. But music was a far more serious business. You could have fun with that, too, but their reputations depended on music. It wasn't a side game, it was the main gig.

At Stankonia they worked with engineer John Frye, who'd been part of the team since 1994 and was used to their style.

"My biggest thing with being in the room with them is that no matter what they say, the answer is yes," John commented.

Experimentation, as always, was the order of the day. One thing could easily lead to another and create a completely new track. That, in fact, happened as they worked on the disc. As they worked on a track, they threaded the tape upside down and played it back, giving something entirely new, which would become the basis for "Ms. Jackson," the song that would prove to be their biggest yet.

Although Big Boi said that "when we go in the studio, we go in with, like, ideas and concepts of different songs. We went in and we like 'Okay, we gonna make an album like this.' We just go in and we work, and whatever comes, comes." When asked, Dre and Big Boi admitted that sometimes as much as eighty percent of a disc can result from improvisation in the studio.

It came from their feelings, recent experiences, ideas, and "just making the best music we can make of that time," as Dre put it. Influences abounded, of course—virtually the only thing you wouldn't find somewhere on an OutKast album was country music.

The balance between the pair kept the music good and even. Both were creative and tamed each other's excesses, while at the same time pushed each other further. They acted as springboards and editors, with a kind of communication and shorthand that developed over the years.

The way they worked, writing and creating tracks in the studio, meant that the recording process took longer than it would have if they'd arrived with virtually completed tracks and rhymes. But it also added a vital spontaneity and edge to the music that made it more immediate and urgent—and that only added to its appeal. Every OutKast album was like walking a tightrope and trying to keep the balance without tumbling off.

That was another reason for the two-year gaps between albums. The way they worked demanded a lot of them, and they needed time away to reach the point where they could stir up the juices and come up with something absolutely fresh each time.

But that was also part of the joy. Their aim with this new disc was, Dre explained, to "shock the hip-hop community, anybody who listens to music, because [music's gotten] kind of boring. We wanted to revive it, kind of like church; a hip-hop Holy Ghost. We're in the age of keeping it real, but what we're trying to do is keep it surreal. Real has gotten really boring. I want to see it done in a fly way, you know what I'm saying?"

Those were high goals, but on the basis of their last two discs, not at all out of the realm of possibility for OutKast. They had the power and the ideas. And at this stage, it was guaranteed that anything they released would be listened to very carefully indeed. Every note, every beat, every word was *important*.

"Whatever you say about us, our shit gonna be funky and the beat's gonna be hard. I don't give a fuck about anything after that," said Big Boi dryly.

After being delayed several times, OutKast's latest offering, the strangely titled *Stankonia* (keeping up a tradition of weirdly named albums) appeared in stores on Halloween, October 31, 2000.

" 'Stankonia,' " Dre said, was "a word we made up joking around . . . you know, if it's stank, it's good, it's funky. 'Stankonia' is the place, the capital we want to bring listeners to."

And this time out they certainly cranked up the funk—and everything else. Within a month the album had gone double platinum, propelled by the single "Ms. Jackson," their first song to go into heavy rotation on MTV. In December the song topped both the *Billboard* R&B/Hip-hop Singles & Tracks chart (for two weeks) and the R&B/Hip-hop Airplay chart (for six weeks). The following month it landed in the main Top 40, and by February it was number one—the first time OutKast had managed that particular distinction—even as the album skipped to triple platinum within four months of its release—a staggering achievement for any hip-hop disc.

As Big Boi noted, "Music is universal."

"Ms. Jackson," of course, was the happy accident that happened when they played a tape upside down in the studio. But from that germ came a superb slice of hip-hop with a hook so big it could catch anything. The singing still favored the falsetto sounds of Curtis Mayfield and Al Green, seductive and beautiful, and absolutely made to be sung along with.

But the verses made everyone sit up and take notice. While the song was seen as Dre's apology to Erykah Badu's mother (who joked that she should receive royalties from the sales), since Dre and Erykah had gone their separate ways, it has to be remembered that Antwan now had two children of his own, Jordan and Bamboo, and by most reports he wasn't part of a couple (the children lived with him). So it stood equally as his apology.

What was so startling was the very act of apology. It was unexpected, a penance for something that hadn't worked out, hurting the women involved—although obviously the men were hurt, too. But along with the apology came an assertion of rights and a promise to take the responsibility for the children involved.

In a time where so many girls were becoming single parents, and so many men were denying responsibility—both financial and emotional—for the children they'd helped bring into the world, it was a dramatic, mature gesture. And it certainly went against the stereotypes of hip-hop, recasting men as equal partners in a family—albeit a family that was no longer together.

The video worked as an analogy for the song. An older woman drove by the ramshackle house where Dre and Big Boi lived. In her wake came a storm that blew up a car, then water poured through leaks in the roof—and a frayed electrical system ending up taking out part of the roof. But when it seemed like the house might be completely destroyed, the storm passed, with blue sky taking its place. In other words, there was hope for the future; it wasn't all bleak.

The video (and the song, obviously) was a contradiction of hip-hop conventions, but it was done to perfection. It brought the band an MTV Video Music Award for Best Hip-hop Video in September 2001 and also a nomination for Best Direction for its director, F. Gary Gray. The song was also powerful enough to garner OutKast's first Grammy in February 2002, for Best Rap Performance by a Duo or Group. However, it wouldn't be the only one Big Boi and Dre would take home that night, as they also walked away with the Best Rap Album award for *Stankonia*, in addition to performing at the ceremony.

The way "Ms. Jackson" was received boded well for the whole album. And though Dre and Antwan were on tenterhooks prior to its release, admitting that there was a buzz about the disc, but they weren't sure how it would be received. As it turned out, they didn't need to worry. Both *Spin* and *Rolling Stone*, two widely read and respected magazines, albeit ones that weren't really associated with hip-hop, called it a "masterpiece."

Certainly it broke down the barriers of hip-hop once and for all. There was the guitar-driven fury of "Gasoline Dreams," the laid-back, sophisticated funk of "So Fresh, So Clean," the outraged black rock that was "B.O.B. (Bombs Over Baghdad)," and the desperate story of "Toilet Tisha," among any number of treasures. From humor to serious situations to outright anger, it was all there.

Plenty of people guested on the record. There was a total of fifteen, including an appearance from Erykah Badu on "Humble Mumble." Although she and Dre had gone their separate ways, this seemed to underline the lack of animosity between them). But in each case, the guests brought something special to the party. They weren't there for their names (in several cases they were unknown); they'd been asked along for the specific talents they possessed. It wasn't about ego; it was about making the very best possible record OutKast could make. As they progressed, they were learning about their own limitations and how to ask others for help.

One song that had its beginnings during the sessions was "Hey Ya!" Originally titled "Thank God for Mom and Dad," it began as a raw beat and a guitar line—in fact, the first chords Dre ever learned on guitar. It came after Dre began listening to punk and indie bands like the Ramones, Buzzcocks, and The Smiths, music he'd never heard before. The prototype version of the song, however, while intended for *Stankonia*, never developed in the way the band had hoped, and it was shelved for later. In retrospect, that had to be a good thing.

And it wasn't as if *Stankonia* was short of prime material. Everything on the album was completely developed. They weren't afraid to court some political controversy this time around, either. "B.O.B. (Bombs Over Baghdad)" was a song about the bombing raids on the Iraqi capital in the late 1990s (when the United States was under the Clinton Administration, before George Bush, Jr., was elected, and the whole Iraqi War of 2003). The raids were never intended to achieve much, neither war nor peace; they were simply a signal that the United States was out there watching. To Dre, that hooked up with what he saw as little dedication on the part of so many in the music business to the music itself. There was no heart to so many of the sounds and records they were hearing.

"There were lots of people making music," he pointed out, "but there was nothing real about it. We were like saying, 'Make music that has something to say or just get out of the way.'"

The energized song, which owed a lot to black rock bands like Living Color, laid down the viewpoint firmly, while being decidedly loud and abrasive, especially in its beats, which did bang exactly the way they said on the hook. It was underlined by a highly stylized video, where Dre looked like a cross between Jimi Hendrix and '60s soul man Sly Stone, psychedelic in the extreme, as was the video itself, notable not only for its use of Cadillacs, but especially for the colorization of purple and green grass, before taking the whole thing to church—which, after all, was one of the roots of black music in America.

Once a song is out, however, it takes on a life of its own. Although it seemed as though "B.O.B." had vanished off the radar by 2003, it hadn't. The track became popular with the troops who were over in Iraq; in fact, it became their rallying cry.

The problem was that Big Boi had been against the unilateral use of force by the coalition; he had been vocal in his feelings that the United States should have gone through the United Nations for a mandate to use force in Iraq. But events had happened without that, and now OutKast's song had become an anthem. While he wasn't totally happy about it, he also felt that he had to support the troops who were out there, so "if the song helps them keep their spirits up, I don't have a problem with that."

It was hardly the first time a song had been misinterpreted. Bruce Springsteen's "Born in the U.S.A.," a song that spoke of hardship, had been appropriated as a political anthem in the 1980s, its meaning turned upside down to become a patriotic anthem. When something like this happens, it leaves artists in a tricky spot. Their work has been taken out of context, but they have to live with it. All that OutKast could do was make the most of a situation they couldn't have foreseen at the time they wrote the track.

The criticism of the song and the government policy were quite explicit in the song, enough that neither Dre nor Big Boi felt it needed an explanation. And no matter what they said, people would put their own spin on it anyway. But it wasn't the only song where they had harsh words. "Red Velvet," for example, railed against the huge streak of materialism in hip-hop, where the conspicuous consumption by rappers constantly pushed the ante. Although Dre and Big Boi were doing well financially, they kept everything under control, refusing to go to extremes like so many other artists. They lived well, but quietly. And they still took the advice of their families and invested for the future. Unlike so many who lived and died by the gun, they were definitely planning futures for themselves.

Stankonia was an album to startle even before it was played. The cover featured the pair standing before the Stars and Stripes, but the flag was black and white, not red, white, and blue. The reason, said Dre (who was restyled as Andre 3000 beginning with this album), was "The way I see it, the youth is kinda, like, dead. The black and white represents the deadness of America. So we're just trying to crank it."

And once you put it in the CD player, the ideas ratcheted up from there. "Gasoline Dreams" was about the failure of the American Dream for so many people, especially the band's core constituency, black youth. The laid-back "So Fresh, So Clean" celebrated the virtues of being clean and well dressed, which wasn't too strange, given OutKast's long fascination with fashion.

Along with the bleak "Toilet Tisha," concerning a teenage girl who committed suicide after learning she was pregnant, in a stripped-down song, there was also "Red Velvet," the excoriating look at the state of hip-hop and the way rappers live, elevating themselves above the rest of society.

Writing always began as a personal act for Andre, exploring his own feelings and experiences.

"And then sometimes, we get into songs where I see someone

else in the situation, like being a news reporter, just reporting and trying to feel what somebody else feel." That was something he'd begun doing more and more, and it was most evident on one song from the *Stankonia* sessions that didn't make the cut for the album, but ended up on the soundtrack for the movie *Tomb Raider*.

"Speedballin' " was inspired by the death of the younger brother of an old friend of Andre's, who "got shot out there slangin' dope and all that type of stuff right there, and he was maybe, like, fifteen or fourteen or something like that." But it wasn't a straight antidrug song. It was also an examination of *why* kids were out on the corners doing that. The answer, of course, was that they wanted what other people had, the consumer items advertised on television that were the good life in America.

Did "Ms. Jackson" come from the imagination, from putting themselves in someone else's shoes, or was that one of the personal songs? Andre 3000 admitted that "it's kinda like a personal song, but then at the same time, it's not like a real-life story like that."

And did they succeed in finding the funk on *Stankonia*? They believed so. Big Boi thought it deserved "seven mics, or six." Andre was more thoughtful, saying all they could do was "just put it out there and just pray that the people connect with it."

The reviewers loved it all. *Interview* called it "a whiplash-inducing trip to the funhouse" where the band sounded "like they're experimenting not out of some theoretical interest in being different but because it feels good." *Newsweek* deemed it "an exercise in risk-taking." *Entertainment Weekly* advised people to "take a deep breath and jump into this music," praising the way "Benjamin and Patton shift with dizzyingly assured fluidity between the real and the surreal." And in *The New York Times*, Jon Pareles noted that "bumping and grinding, slipping and sliding, OutKast's music savors the viscous propulsion of funk, with raps and tunes that never ignore the body and its instinctive desires."

One of the centerpieces of the record was the brief track "?" The song was a hard, fast series of questions that wondered about the behavior of African-Americans and the way they treated each other, perpetrating violence on each other. They weren't the first people to ask these questions, by any means. But to say them loudly to such a wide audience put them completely in the face of the public. And by doing that, they could make people look inside and wonder about the answers.

Stankonia arrived just as rock-rap became an important commercial musical subgenre. Acts like Limp Bizkit had sold a lot of records, especially with their most recent album, *Chocolate Starfish and the Hot Dog Flavored Water*. The more politically charged Rage Against the Machine used rhymes alongside their metal to volatile effect.

Notably, the artists pushing rock-rap were white bands, although when the first record in the style emerged, in 1986, it was a true collaboration between rappers Run-D.M.C. and hard rockers Aerosmith on the song "Walk This Way."

OutKast represented the other side of the equation, the black perspective on it all. They could rock as hard as anyone on the planet, banging the beats and pouring electric guitars all over the mix, as they did on "Gasoline Dreams" and "B.O.B.," where the playing owed so much to Parliament/Funkadelic's six-string wizard, Eddie Hazel, who in turn had Jimi Hendrix as an inspiration. They could funk like Sly Stone or Prince, both of whom had mixed up rock and funk in very strong proportions.

Unlike so many rock-rappers, though, Andre and Big Boi also understood that a song had to have a groove. Without that, you had nothing except noise. The groove helped establish the flow, and they'd become masters of the flow, whether it was a laid-back jam like "So Fresh, So Clean" or the manic intentions of "Gasoline Dreams."

On top of that, rapping was something they understood innately. They'd grown up with it, it had been their lives for a full decade since they'd met. It was what they did, and everything else had come later. With OutKast, the rock built on the hip-hop base, not the other way around. And that gave it the kind of soulful foundation that bands like Limp Bizkit couldn't achieve.

Perhaps the most important fact was that OutKast was continually questing. It simply wasn't in the band's nature to just sit back and copy others. Big Boi and Andre had to be constantly innovating in a way most bands might wish, but could rarely achieve. After the raves that had greeted *Aquemini*, the easy and obvious route would have been to make another album that sounded similar and give the world time to catch up. But things evolved at a hectic pace, and standing still wasn't even an option—it wasn't even considered.

Stankonia also featured the best integration between live instruments and electronics that the band had achieved, which could have been attributable to the fact that they handled so much of the production themselves. Curious little things bubbled in and out of the mix, like the '80s electro-synthesizer line that popped up during "B.O.B.," then vanished again.

There was a frantic energy to much of the album and an urgency that hadn't been evident on the earlier discs. Maybe that was due to the fact that the pair felt they had more to say this time around. It would be easy to pigeonhole this as their "social" album, full of concerns, but that would be facile. At twenty-five, and as parents, they were both naturally concerned with the outside world—and their places in it. They were stars who lived in relatively privileged circumstances. They'd never be short of money. But that didn't stop their righteous anger.

It didn't stop the fun, either, as they showed in the interludes. "Cruisin' in the ATL" was a few seconds of early '80s funk. "Kim & Cookie," although X-rated for its language, skewered the attitudes of some girl in a hilarious fashion. And "Pre-Nump" poked fun at the lack of romance in marriage. Even the cheesy back of the CD booklet was an acknowledgment of the tacky covers of so many cheap soul records from the '60s and '70s.

Above all, the album really was funky. Even "Gangsta Sh*t," a careful dissection of the irrelevance of the whole gangsta and thug style, funked like crazy. It was with good reason that they began referring to themselves as the "coolest motherfunkers on the planet." At this point they just may have been. Coming out of hip-hop, they'd picked up the mantle of artists like Prince to make music that was both sincere and funky. Their ear for a hook and chorus had continued to develop, too, with "Ms. Jackson" a perfect case in point. Truthfully, though, there were several tracks on *Stankonia* that could have made excellent singles, although sometimes the subject matter weighed against that possibility.

That did bring up another issue, which was how OutKast handled the issue of language. There was plenty of cursing on their records, and there had been from the beginning. It was a part of everyday language—and the flow of that language—for them, and they'd seen no reason to tone it down, because that would have altered who they were. But when it came to singles, they had to be willing to make some compromises. Radio wasn't going to play tracks with a lot of swearing. Rather than have words either bleeped out or simply not there, they sometimes preferred to rere-cord with slightly altered lyrics for singles. The whole idea of "clean" and "dirty" versions was just beginning to come into play, where it was possible to buy either the original or expurgated ver-sions of albums. That made for a lot more work, obviously, but also meant that kids whose parents wouldn't have allowed them to own the more adult versions now had access to the work. Yes, it increased the possible fan base, but the band was watering down their music, selling out their original artistic intentions, at least according to some of their hard-core followers. In general, the clean versions simply cut out objectionable language. But Big Boi noted the hypocrisy behind the censorship.

"They're trying to blame violence on music. Take the movies, for instance. Some movies are the most violent shit out. You can't even show people getting pistol-whipped in videos or any-thing, but in movies you can show everything."

It was a good, strong point. Language alone couldn't kill, but it was seen as more insidious and dangerous than watching vio-lence (much the same applied to sex, too). It showed that people were scared of words and their power—and words, after all, were a rapper's tools and weapons, to be used sharply and carefully.

Notably in the video for "Ms. Jackson," the offensive lan-guage was just edited out, and again for "So Fresh, So Clean," whose bright colors and uplifting vibe were enough to sustain it.

OutKast might no longer have been of the street, but they still knew plenty of people who were, their homies from East Point. And it wasn't that long ago that they'd been out there themselves. They still understood what it was like and needed to address those people just as much—if not more—than any other segment of their audience and do it in their own language, although much of that language had become ubiquitous in young America.

By the time OutKast hit the road in support of *Stankonia*, their star had completely ascended. They'd had a number-one single, and the album itself was triple platinum. They'd graduated from clubs to arenas, and from support act to major headliner. There was more to the tour than simply jumping onstage, delivering the hits, and leaving for the hotel. OutKast featured a real well-rehearsed stage show that required a specially designed stage set.

The band appeared onto what looked remarkably like a cave; certainly it was nothing from the modern world with its collection of stalactites and picket fences. And they really pushed the guitar-fueled aspect of their music by having not one but two guitarists playing live, along with two backup singers—a necessity, given the way their music had gone far beyond rap—and a DJ to provide the beats and backing. There were also four male dancers, who were only on for a fraction of the set.

And what a set! After opening acts Ludacris (another Atlanta homeboy) and L.A. rapper Xzibit, who'd just gone platinum with *Restless*, it was one hundred nonstop minutes of OutKast. Considering the fact that Andre 3000 hated to tour, when he was up there he gave it his all. Kicking off each night with "Gasoline Dreams," they powered through it all, moving quickly from song to song rather than indulging in a lot of talking to the audience.

They'd learned a lot about using the stage since their early appearances after the first album. By now they were relatively seasoned road veterans, and Big Boi reveled in the traveling and the shows. They steered carefully away from the hip-hop clichés like banal choreography or call-and-response with the audience.

The people had paid their money to be entertained, and the band made sure they went home satisfied.

The pace was hot throughout, and they ran through material from all four of their albums to date. Given that they'd really broken through with the newest one, Andre couldn't resist a little dig at those who'd just discovered them when he said, "I bet there's a lot of people that think *Stankonia* is our first album," before they headed into the title cut from *Southernplayalisticadillacmuzik.*

They were as funky live as they were on record, which was quite an achievement. There was no way they could be as subtle, given the environment and changing acoustics of concert venues, but they did their best.

Of course, Andre did his best to provide a visual feast, the peacock against Big Boi's slightly more conservative outfits. Unfortunately, as *The Washington Post* noted, the lighting designer seemed to want to light everything from behind the stage, which "turned everyone onstage into little more than a silhouette." The addition of plenty of strobe lights—an unnecessary way to amp up the excitement—made it something of an assault on the eyes at times.

Curiously, or perhaps perversely, given the recent huge increase in their audience, they only played about half the songs off *Stankonia*, giving ample, gleeful airings to a lot of older material to an audience largely unfamiliar with the songs. In fact, they made them wait until late in the show for the tune so many had come to hear, "Ms. Jackson." It was a wise move, making sure that the crowd would stay that long. And at the Patriot Center in Washington, D.C., once that song had been played, quite a few headed to the exits, berated by Andre to "Sit your [behinds] back down!"

One thing OutKast had always emphasized in their music

was positive movement. They'd shown how the gangsta path was nothing more than a dead end, albeit a glamorous one. And in the wake of several shootings at high schools around the country, they decided to take their own positive steps. They teamed with the Nike Youth Action program to help bring about change.

It was a given that kids were often scared to speak up about things at school, things that could help prevent shootings, simply because of peer pressure and the natural reluctance of teenagers.

The program OutKast got behind was to give grants to non-profit youth groups to bring in speakers who might make the kids realize the futility in remaining silent. Additionally, Out-Kast was set to visit the youth groups on nine stops of their tour (out of a total of forty dates) and talk to the kids themselves, emphasizing the need for youth activism. It was a move sure to draw teenagers, especially since they were also handing out free concert tickets, and they planned on bringing a representative from each youth group onstage at their shows.

It all served to make the tour about more than music. Putting their money (and also their time) on the line showed they were serious about it all. There'd been no one to do those kinds of things when they were younger, and as parents themselves, they understood the responsibility of adults—especially stars—as role models for the young.

The tour was a complete success, there was no doubt about that. But to Andre it felt more like an obligation than any kind of fun. He loved creating music, that was for certain, but performing it night after night and the stress of traveling from city to city, hotel to venue to hotel, then back on the road, wasn't something he relished.

It was, if you will, the ongoing contrast of the poet and the player. Andre preferred the surroundings of home and the studio, more settled environments where he was in control. On the other hand, Big Boi loved life on the road, where he was feted and indulged.

Again, even on tour, they never went over the top. They traveled by bus, rather than plane, and only used a small crew. Their real extravagance was the stage set, which was vital in this day and age to put on a real show.

Back at home, when the road time was over and they'd both had a chance to decompress, it was time to begin thinking about something new—which was exactly what they didn't want to do. They needed time to recharge their batteries and consider the possibilities for the future. Andre's thoughts had begun to move toward acting, a new field to conquer. He'd even started taking lessons on saxophone and clarinet, two instruments not generally associated with hip-hop, but a reflection of the fact that his interests had spread far from their beginnings.

There was also talk of him looking into acting, although that idea was still in its infancy. But it was evident that Andre was starting to feel restless. For the last four years Andre had been gradually breaking out and doing the unexpected, so whatever moves he made wouldn't be too surprising.

Big Boi, on the other hand, seemed very content with his life. Pitfall Kennels was established and, thanks in part to his celebrity, there was no shortage of customers for the puppies. They no longer bred only pit bulls, there were also rottweilers and English bulldogs among the breeds. But pit bulls were still the focus.

Pitfall Kennels remains a family business. Big Boi helps out at times, although most of the work is done by his brother James, while yet another younger brother, Marcus, drives out some mornings to help clean and exercise the dogs.

They've achieved something that is the goal of many breeding kennels—they've established a Pitfall bloodline, the rare "blue" pit bull, which had been established by careful, selective breeding.

While pit bulls had reputations as vicious fighting dogs, Big Boi insists they are no more dangerous than any other breed, and he certainly isn't about to let his prized animals go against others in a ring.

"The dogs come out so beautiful," he says. "Put 'em in a ring and they get scarred for life—for what?"

Considering the fact that Big Boi started the business by asking advice from some dog trainers and sitting down with "the Purina books for kenneling," he's come a long way very quickly. With the puppies selling for large amounts, it is also a lucrative business. He has his dogs registered through the United Kennel Club and the American Dog Breeders Association; this is definitely more than just a rapper's hobby.

INTO THE
6. UNKNOWN

IN THE wake of albums that grew bigger and bigger, the real wonder was where OutKast would go next. They were contracted to make more albums, and they would honor that, obviously, but for now creating something new was low on their priority list.

In the meantime, there was one obvious choice, to put out a "best-of" disc. And like most modern single artist compilations, it would contain some unreleased tracks. That way not only would new fans who'd only heard OutKast on the radio buy it, but people who'd been into them since the beginning would also purchase the album, just to make sure they had those new cuts.

While they preferred to call it a "refresher course" for their fans, *Big Boi & Dre Present . . . OutKast* really was a hits collection. Obviously it covered all the big songs and all four albums very well, from "Player's Ball" onward.

It also served another purpose. Coming a bit more than a year after *Stankonia*, it kept interest in the band high and also arrived just in time for Christmas shoppers in 2001—in other words, fairly standard record company policy.

Southernplayalisticadillacmuzik was represented not only by "Player's Ball," but also by the title cut, the excellent "Crumblin' Erb," the motivated "Git Up, Git Out," and, surprisingly, "Ain't No Thang." Perhaps it spoke volumes about the accessibility of the disc that only the hit "Elevators (Me & You)" was pulled from *ATLiens*—both the title track and "Jazzy Belle" (which had been released as singles) would have fitted well. *Aquemini* fared better, as "Aquemini," "Spottieottiedopalicious," and, of course, "Rosa Parks" all made the cut, while *Stankonia* contributed the ubiquitous "Ms. Jackson," "B.O.B.," and "So Fresh, So Clean."

It was intentionally heavy on the songs with mass appeal, with little or no emphasis on OutKast's experimental side. But that was the nature of collections like this. The three new tracks—or, at least, not previously released—were "Funkin' Around," "The Whole World," where they worked with one of their protégés, Killer Mike, and "Movin' Cool (the After Party)," a slower jazz club type jam to end things. There was also the new "Intro," but that didn't exactly count as a musical track.

The new tracks weren't outstanding, certainly not OutKast at its very best, but they were still good—Andre and Big Boi weren't about to sully their reputation by releasing anything that wasn't good. "Funkin' Around" was heavy on the brass, but the real winner was "The Whole World," which laid down the P-Funk very heavily and let Killer Mike loose on the microphone.

It was the obvious choice for a single and proved to be a good one.

Just as it came out, OutKast was back in the news again, topping *Billboard*'s year-end chart for 2001 as Top Hip-hop/R&B Album Artists for the sales of *Stankonia*. They'd also managed five Grammy nominations, which meant they should walk away with at least one, if not more.

And, as if to prove that anything with the OutKast name attached could do no wrong, "The Whole World" slid right into the Top 40 in February 2001, a month before *Big Boi & Dre Present . . . OutKast* turned platinum.

Maybe the Grammy Awards were important to OutKast; maybe they weren't. One thing was a certainty, however. If they walked off with an award, it would translate into more record sales. The fact that they were also performing at the ceremony meant they'd be very visible on the night itself.

They'd been nominated for Best Rap Performance by a Duo or Group, Best Rap Album, Album of the Year, Record of the Year, and Best Music Video, Short Form. The real prizes were Album of the Year and Record of the Year, which received the most attention because they were the most important awards.

It was impossible not to get caught up in all the drama that accompanied the awards. And there were plenty of people who wanted OutKast to walk away with a fistful of Grammys at the Staples Center in Los Angeles.

That wasn't going to happen. There was plenty of stiff competition. No one was too astonished when the soundtrack to the movie *O Brother, Where Art Thou?* took home Album of the Year honors. The film, a surprising runaway success, had revitalized the interest of America in its roots music. The soundtrack would go several times platinum, giving a real boost to roots music—which desperately needed it.

U2 had the Record of the Year, with "Walk On" from *All That You Can't Leave Behind*, which was also Rock Album of the Year. It was the year of their renaissance, when they came back fully into the public eye.

The Short Form Video award ended up with Fatboy Slim and Bootsy Collins for "Weapon of Choice," which had been directed by Spike Jonze, one of the most imaginative and very best of the younger music video directors.

However, OutKast did claim two Grammy Awards—Best Rap Performance and Record of the Year—and performed, which meant they were very visible in Los Angeles that night. And even if they weren't the two biggest awards, it was recognition from the industry that they were doing something right. Those years down in the Dungeon and in Stankonia Studios certainly hadn't been wasted.

In some ways, it was surprising that the daring experimentation that was *Stankonia* won. But there was also a logic to it: The album offered realistic messages and didn't try to glorify the thug lifestyle, unlike so many other major hip-hop albums. The messages transcended the music—or at least complemented it. And no one who'd been moved by what they said doubted the award was fully justified.

OutKast was at the top of the heap. They'd walked away with a coveted prize: the award for the best rap CD of the year. But as always the big question was: What next? After four albums together had Big Boi and Andre taken OutKast, and their musical relationship, as far as possible?

They'd been called the Beatles of hip-hop, but even that writing partnership of John Lennon and Paul McCartney ended. And certainly neither of them had thought that OutKast might last forever.

As usual, they took a break following the Grammy Awards, a time to think and look around. At least, with their best-of disc selling so well, there was no immediate pressure on them to come up with a new record; they were off the hook for another year.

Yet they remained firmly in the spotlight as other awards came thick and fast. In March 2002 there was a World Music Award for being the world's best-selling rap group. In June, at the BET Awards, they walked away as Best Group. October brought the *GQ* Men of the Year Awards, where they were named Band Men of the Year. And while they didn't win, they were nominated for Best Hip-hop Video at the MTV Video Music Awards for "The Whole World."

Andre's interests in instruments outside the hip-hop realm were a mirror of his restlessness. His personality was such that he was considering moving into acting—which would mean shifting his base to Los Angeles, the home of films. That was a big step. He was an urbane sophisticate with a fuzzy edge these days, but he was still a Southerner born and bred. Could he handle the Wild West on a permanent basis?

Big Boi, meanwhile, remained very much committed to Out-Kast. He'd already been back into Stankonia Studios to begin work on what he planned as their next album. He was more focused than his partner, perhaps, but equally experimental in his approach. Of course, that had always been the joy of Out-Kast, their willingness to color outside the lines. And having their own studio, Big Boi could experiment whenever and however he wanted. But for now, he was mostly doing it alone.

They'd actually been considering working together but separately for a while. As early as March 2001, Andre 3000 suggested in an interview that their next disc might be a double, with one CD from each of them, along with a few songs they did together. The main reason, he insisted at the time, was that the single-disc format was simply too small to contain all their ideas.

Rumors about OutKast floated around continually. At one point it was said that Andre would front a live funk band, but he nixed that, just as he insisted OutKast would never use a full band for backing on live dates.

He did drop hints, however, that in addition to the clothing line, there might soon be a movie with OutKast.

Now, over a year later, the clothing line continued to expand, but the movie idea seemed to have fallen by the wayside; at the very least, it wasn't being mentioned anymore. That didn't mean it was forgotten; it had simply been transferred to the back burner.

Movies remained at the forefront of Andre's mind, however. For all his outlandish colorful clothes and occasionally left-field ideas, he was grounded enough to realize he wasn't going to suddenly take the movie business by storm and walk in as a star. That was why, when he was offered a bit part in a film, he jumped at the chance to get his foot in the door.

The movie was *Hollywood Homicide*, a vehicle for veteran Harrison Ford and Josh Harnett. Its working title had been *Two Cops* when Andre signed on, and it revolved, at least in part, around the murder of a rapper, making it an ideal fit. Andre (going under his real name of Andre Benjamin) had a very small part as screenwriter Silky Brown—a much larger role went to New Orleans-based Master P, playing Julius Armas.

While the reviews would be very mixed when it appeared in 2003, the fact remained that he'd been in a movie, and Andre had the taste to do more film work. He liked the laid-back vibe of the West Coast and its lifestyle, not to mention all the beautiful women around.

Films grew from projects and ideas. Often just having the nugget, rather than even a full script, could bring the financing. Certainly the idea of an independent film also appealed to Andre. And that was just as well, when he was contacted to act in one and also to create the music for it.

This was very much his chance to step outside the musical mold of OutKast and create music that was utterly different, that had nothing to do with hip-hop. He'd been searching for the opportunity to spread his wings—and this was it.

Andre had also begun listening to a lot of jazz, anything from the inspiration of the groundbreaking John Coltrane albums of the 1960s to the Crusaders, who helped smooth jazz out in the '70s. This helped to explain Andre's earlier preoccupations with the saxophone and clarinet. Andre's interest in jazz seemed to be growing.

Where he'd go with his new music remained to be seen, but he was definitely excited by the opening of the new vistas ahead of him. Not only did it bring in his base—music—but it also combined it with his new love of films.

With Big Boi in Atlanta and Andre in L.A., the pair were working on completely different projects. However, that wasn't completely new. Much of *Stankonia* had been done individually.

Then they'd play their tracks to each other and work on them together. This time, it seemed, there'd be no collaboration.

Andre 3000 could work quickly when he wanted to, and in short order he had five tracks ready as movie music, including "The Love Below," which the movie people liked so much they decided to name the movie after it—a very encouraging sign.

It was really only at that point that Andre realized he was in the middle of a solo album. Knowing that his partner was also at work, he came up with the idea of them releasing solo discs. But Big Boi didn't like that, and neither did their manager. It made sense: OutKast was a big name, but Andre 3000 and Big Boi weren't in the same league. They needed at least another smash before they charged off into solo careers.

"They didn't want me to drop a solo album before the next OutKast album," Andre said. "I was kind of upset. At first I was gonna release 'em on the Internet and just give it away for free."

The whole game changed when the movie Dre was recording the soundtrack for fell apart. It was a matter of financing, really; the promised money simply didn't materialize.

By that time Dre had several completed tracks. So did Big Boi, who was working at a much brisker pace at Stankonia Studios. In fact, by February 2003 his album was complete. He wanted the new OutKast disc released, so he could get out on the road. But Andre 3000 was far from ready. His ideas were constantly changing and evolving. He was even changing studios on a regular basis, commuting back to Atlanta to work at Stankonia Studios with engineer John Frye, who'd been part of the team for almost a decade.

The way Andre and Big Boi worked was completely different, according to Frye. With Andre, they'd record "many tracks of overdubs of guitars, maybe vocals, basses, different sounds, and we'd try to get it all down while he's in the creative mode, and then more or less weed it out later." Big Boi, on the other hand, liked to begin with the beat, and "even if some other producer brought in a beat, he'd often take it to the OutKast level with whatever he was feeling or talking about."

Andre relied far more heavily on live playing and musicians, and it was apparent early on that his was going to be a vocal, rather than rap, album.

Experimentation continued to be the order of the day. Andre's "She Lives in My Lap" began as a guitar jam, then took off in a different direction as the track was being laid down in the studio—a direction that was eagerly pursued, resulting in the completed song. The multitrack version of the song was also reversed, and then became something completely different, the track "Vibrate"—two songs for the price of one, if you like, much in the manner of "Ms. Jackson."

While Andre worked wildly, Big Boi was more methodical. He'd go through the original tracking of beats and instruments, then the vocals and overdubs, the rough mix, and the final mix. And by that final mix, everything was already virtually finished; it was more down to tweaking than anything else.

That didn't mean it was any less inspired, simply more straight ahead, as Big Boi entered with a more complete vision of what he wanted, where Andre was liable to take off on wild tangents, such as the version of "My Favorite Things." Based on the famous John Coltrane version of the classic Oscar Hammerstein tune, it took the jazz trio, with saxophone (not Andre's playing) improvising around the melody, then added a skittering jungle rhythm underneath. Given that Andre had been listening to a lot of Coltrane (and studying saxophone), it was an obvious homage to a hero, but modernized in a way that made it

Andre and Big Boi burn it up onstage.

(JEFF MAYER)

Andre takes on military chic.

Ten years on and the sounds keep getting better.
Andre and Big Boi, still together. (JEFF MAYER)

**Always dapper . . . this time with their
Soul Train Awards** (VINNIE ZUFFANTE)

A man needs a cigar . . . Big Boi and Chinese symbol.

Even the red carpet is a chance for performance.

Dressing high and dressing low for the
Billboard Awards [VINNIE ZUFFANTE]

The fruits of "Hey Ya!" . . . a fistful of Grammy Awards

(JEFF MAYER)

cool to a younger audience, turning the whole thing around and reinventing what had become a jazz standard, both as a tune and in execution.

Once again, both Andre and Big Boi brought in guests to help out, more than they had on *Stankonia* or *Aquemini*, although Frye claimed "there are actually fewer guest appearances than ever before." There was an art to it all, and the Out-Kast pair were the musicians/painters who looked at each song as a canvas. Just because they used other people didn't diminish their own talent. Instead it enhanced it with fresh textures and colors.

One interesting point is that most of the instruments recorded on the discs were recorded "dry," that is without processing or effects. About the only exception was the guitar solo on "Prototype," and even that was merely sent through a reverb. By modern standards, that was virtually unheard of. The ability to change the sounds of instruments was widely used throughout all genres of music and had become a recording staple, to be reproduced in concert. The result was a very raw, immediate sound, with the kind of warmth not often heard nowadays. And since, like virtually everything in the twenty-first century, it was all recorded digitally (a medium usually thought of as "cold"), that added warmth was welcome, especially given the funkiness of so many of the tracks.

While Big Boi's music continued in the established OutKast tradition, Andre's work-in-progress was far more fluid and indefinable. But as he pointed out, "Originally it wasn't supposed to be catered to the OutKast fan. It wasn't supposed to be the package that I delivered because people know me for rhyming." The movie for which he'd been composing material "was a love story, so these songs made sense."

As 2003 progressed Andre's album still wasn't finished, even as OutKast fulfilled a handful of live dates they'd already agreed to play. Big Boi was becoming frustrated. For a few years now, when they'd toured they'd played around two hundred gigs over the course of a year. He liked life on the road, and now he didn't have that. But Andre was enjoying those live shows less and less. It had reached the point where, when they were out supporting *Stankonia*, "I would be onstage going through the motions while performing every night. I was totally distant from what I was doing. It was like I was watching myself. There was no passion in it at all. The last show at the University of Georgia was when I knew that I couldn't really keep doing this until I found something that I was passionate about again."

For their new shows, they actually performed separately—the first time they'd done that. Of course, that only brought back the old speculation that they were splitting up—ideas that didn't sound too strange now that they'd been recording individually, too. But they were still quick to dispel any of that. OutKast was a tighter bond than recording or performing, it was a friendship that dated back thirteen years, all the way to high school. And it was also a business partnership, with the band obligated to deliver three more albums to Arista, the parent company of LaFace.

Andre's new material wasn't all new, in fact. "Hey Ya!" had its beginnings in the early sessions for *Stankonia*, and a few other songs had originally been written a few years before, then set aside as material that didn't fit OutKast—at least, at the time. His willingness to explore new forms showed in the fact that his whole album only contained two verses of rapping. Instead, more than ever, the emphasis was on melody and voices, whether from Norah Jones on the acoustic duet "Take Off Your Cool" or his own singing, which was all over the disc. Andre didn't consider himself a singer, by any means, but he did admit that he was "a melody maker."

Satisfying as the whole creative and recording process was, his album was just getting finished, and Big Boi's had been ready since February. By now summer had rolled around, and everybody was still waiting for Andre. It wasn't a case of him not having finished the final mixes, either. On some songs there were still entire verses of lyrics he had to write and record. Everything was coming down to the wire in a major way.

Andre admitted it. "Every album I do this. It's just never been this bad." And finally in August it came to the crunch. He had four days left to complete the work. He'd already missed several deadlines, and now it had to be done if the double CD was to appear in September.

By the final week of August, it was panic stations. Andre was in L.A. working in four separate studios at once to finish all the tracks for the album. That involved staying up for four days straight, but finally, in one last burst of energy, it was all done.

Once the tracks are finished—that is, when they've been recorded and mixed to everyone's satisfaction—the process isn't quite complete. Discs still need to be "mastered." For that the tracks are played in a special mastering studio, and final adjustments are made to change the brightness of the sound or other subtle effects that enhance the music without altering it. Only after that can the CDs be pressed, a very speedy process.

Given the fact that OutKast's new disc was in the stores by the end of September, all the artwork and printing had been taken care of before Andre turned in his work. Everything was ready to roll.

Even Big Boi hadn't heard all his partner's tracks before they were completed, which was a very unusual move, given the way they'd relied on each other for input in the past. But these were most definitely solo albums, just put together under the Out-Kast name as Andre had predicted a couple of years earlier. Interestingly, Andre had been involved in some of Big Boi's tracks, sometimes helping write them, and even producing one or two, like the old school "Ghetto Musick." Notably, though, in place of their Earthtone III production company, Andre and Big Boi each had their own production companies these days.

It had been a strange ride to reach this place, but now they had to discover if the end product really worked. More than Antwan, Andre was terrified; after all, he was the one who'd really stepped outside the box in this.

Really, the last few years hadn't been too easy for him. He'd been so busy with recording that it had been difficult to see much of his son, who was still living with his mother in Dallas. Erykah had become involved with the rapper Common, who, because of circumstances, was able to spend more time with Seven than Andre had. And the boy was growing up, learning how to get a reaction from his father. Luckily, the lines of communication between the two parents were still open, and Andre was adult enough to be able to deal with another man in his son's life.

He'd also announced that he simply wasn't going to tour to support the record. Going on the road no longer held any attraction for him. That wouldn't stop Big Boi, who went out in early 2004 as a solo act—perfectly feasible, given that he had a full album of his own material in *Speakerboxxx*. And he couldn't wait to head out and enjoy the tour life on the bus, in the hotels, and most especially onstage.

The original plan had been to release Andre's "She Lives in My Lap" as the album's first single. It was a track he'd completed early, and advance copies of the single had already been sent to radio for airplay (although it hadn't actually been released yet) when Andre sent L. A. Reid, now the head of Arista Records, a rough demo of "Hey Ya!," announcing that he wanted it to be the single.

Reid listened to it and wasn't convinced. That was understandable; it was a song that needed more than one listen to sink in. But, as he said, "a couple of hours later it suddenly jumped into my head again, and I realized, 'My God, this is it!'"

And it certainly was. It was totally unexpected, but in so many ways that was what people wanted from OutKast. And it wasn't a hip-hop single. It was a pop record. For a track that had been around almost four years, it had developed in a strange way. The opening was the kind of New Wave sound that Andre had been listening to as he started *Stankonia*, before it morphed into the irresistible chorus. By all logic, it shouldn't have worked. There was no real song structure to it, to the point where a first listening could be very confusing.

Interestingly, the groove of the track was put together during just a couple of days in the studio—it was one of the last tracks completed for the album—and many of the lines were made up as he went, including the classic "Shake it like a Polaroid picture" (although he admitted having first written that several years before). In an age of digital cameras, the "instant photos" of Polaroid had become a bit passé, most particularly the old technique of shaking the picture to dry it.

Reid was willing to back Andre on the choice of single, curious as it seemed at first. He'd retained his position as a label head, in part, by making the right choices about artists and material and picking winners. He'd learned to trust his instincts, and there was no doubt what they were telling him in this case.

The track was very much an Andre solo affair. He played all the instruments except the bass, for which he recruited Aaron Mills from Cameo, the Atlanta funk band who'd enjoyed a huge hit in the '80s with the song "Word Up!" The only other person on the track was a single female backup singer; Andre handled all the male vocals.

The clever video (for which Andre had to play through the entire song twenty-eight times as it was filmed) reflected the amount of his involvement in the tune. In a sly homage to the Beatles's 1964 appearance on *The Ed Sullivan Show*, which made them into instant stars in America, Andre became a band, playing all the instruments and singing.

It captured what everyone saw as the open, carefree spirit of the song—one of the reasons, apart from its sing-along chorus, that it became so big. It made you feel good. But there was a darker side to it, actually about the complexity of keeping relationships of all kinds together.

"Hey Ya!" did the rarest of all things; it crossed over into every music demographic. Longtime OutKast fans might have been confused by the song, but beyond that, everyone took to it. It was upbeat and poppy. Those who'd grown up on '80s music loved the New Wave references, and even those who were older thought it harked back to the supposed Golden Age of pop music. It was a winner in every possible direction. The video was in heavy rotation on MTV and VH1, and it was all over the radio.

It went straight into the Top 40 and kept climbing, boosted even more when OutKast performed it on *Saturday Night Live* and then the American Music Awards in November, after which it went to number one, where it couldn't be shifted for the next seven weeks.

"Hey Ya!" formed its own little cottage industry. It quickly became the most downloaded ring tone for cell phones. It was parodied many times—one even began the *The 2004 Golden Globe Awards* show. Its sheer ubiquity had made it into a piece of pop culture, which very rarely happens to an individual song.

Having released one of Andre's songs as a single, it was only fair that one of Big Boi's tracks receive the same treatment. Unlike Andre's tracks, which were all over the place, Big Boi's were more firmly in the OutKast mold, although the influence of '80s funk and electro was far more evident this time around.

The song they settled on was "The Way You Move," and in its own way it was every bit as catchy as "Hey Ya!" The rap was a little autobiographical before exploding into a real soul chorus that was the real hook of the piece—just right for dancing.

Releasing two singles almost simultaneously was a highly unusual business move, especially when the first was still climbing the chart. But in this case, there was sense behind it. The two songs were so different, they could have been different artists (in fact, they were, even if they appeared under the Out-Kast name). And it showed in the way they both sold. "The Way You Move" chased up the Top 40, reaching number two in December, giving OutKast the two top places as 2003 ended.

At that point "Hey Ya!" was in pole position on four separate charts, and it was being named as the best single and video of the year all over the place. *Rolling Stone* crowned it, as did the *Village Voice*. It really was the kind of song that came along once in a decade, an accident of genius that completely penetrated the public consciousness. In years to come, it'll show up on classic rock stations and people will remember where they were or who they were with when they first heard it.

"The Way You Move" didn't achieve that, but it did manage to take over the number-one spot from "Hey Ya!" in January and stay there for six weeks, meaning OutKast had managed to spend more than three months at the top with back-to-back top singles, a remarkable feat at any time.

The real test of what OutKast could achieve these days came with the release of their new disc. *Speakerboxxx* was Big Boi's contribution, a nod both to the way the South loved that booming bass (he even called his production company Boom Boom Room Productions) and also to speaking out. It was a hip-hop album, but in the OutKast sense, meaning it drew in plenty of other elements and ratcheted up the funk the way few other rappers could envision, let alone manage. Andre's disc was *The Love Below*, taken from one of the songs he'd written for the abandoned movie. Put them together and you got *Speakerboxxx/The Love Below*.

In both cases, some of the material was older—a simple look at the writing credits showed that. And Andre had been around for some of Big Boi's tracks, producing them for him (Antwan, in turn, rapped on "Roses"). So there was some crossover. However, the vast majority of the material was new.

It was an eagerly awaited disc. Three years had passed since OutKast had released a disc of all-new material, and during

2001 and 2002 their star had continued to rise, with all the awards they'd received. While there was no doubt it would easily pass the platinum mark, there were still plenty of questions. Would fans accept the divergent directions of the pair, especially with Andre's vision being so out there? Could they replicate the success of *Stankonia*? And how would the critics view it?

Additionally, two CDs of material was a lot for anyone to take in, especially with a higher price tag. Would enough people be willing to spend that kind of money? There would be one little bit of help in terms of sales figures, though: For sales purposes, a double CD actually counted as two discs. So going platinum in this case would actually mean half a million copies had been sold, each copy counting twice.

In any event, there was really very little reason to worry. Helped greatly by the immediate popularity of "Hey Ya!" *Speakerboxxx/The Love Below* shot out of the gate in a gratifying way no one could have quite anticipated.

It was the kind of success record companies dream about, but all too rarely get. From the thousands of CDs released in any given year, only a very, very few are real successes. Of course, over the years, the bar measuring success has been gradually raised. Going back, a gold record was a huge sign of achievement. Sometime during the '90s, that grew to platinum, and then, in the wake of a few mega-acts, double or triple platinum. Ultimate success, of course, was much greater, and the music industry was forced to create an elite category above platinum. So "diamond" was invented, indicating sales of more than 10 million of an album. It was quite deliberately exclusive and reserved for a few superstar acts like Britney Spears and Celine Dion.

There were still yardsticks that measured success along the

way. For an album to enter the *Billboard* chart right at the top was one of them, and so was achieving platinum status within a month.

OutKast managed both of those with ease—and actually went one better: Within four weeks it had turned *triple* platinum, with three million units going out of the stores. It was selling like hotcakes.

By November it was four times platinum, and by January 2004, a staggering eight times platinum. Along the way it had managed to become the fifth-biggest selling album of 2003. Considering that it had only been available for the last three months of 2003, that was truly remarkable indeed.

Nor did it stop there. The pace might have slowed, but by March it had risen to nine million copies sold, edging its way to that elusive and desirable diamond status—which it was by now absolutely certain to manage, and sooner rather than later, within a year of its release.

What was the secret? Had America finally caught up with OutKast after all this time, or had the music of Andre and Big Boi changed enough to become widely commercial? The answer was probably a bit of both. Their songwriting had never been better, and their sense of arrangement brimmed with fun. In both cases there was the continuing debt to soul, although no longer the Curtis Mayfield influence that had informed their music in the early years. Now it was easy to spot bits of Prince, for example, in "Roses," touches of Sly and the Family Stone, Marvin Gaye, and several other greats, all seamlessly woven into the fabric that was OutKast. Not just the South, but America as a whole had come to love bass, and the albums had plenty of it.

As much as *Speakerboxxx/The Love Below* was a contemporary album, there was also a very retro feel to it. Vintage synthesizer sounds were all over (it's probably no accident that one of the instruments to be found at Stankonia Studios is a mellotron, a very early type of synthesizer that was used for string sounds in the late 1960s). Both Andre and Antwan had fully assimilated their loves of the past into the present, maybe more successfully than any neo-soul artist currently being written up in magazines. They understood it on an innate, cellular level.

To be fair, they'd changed contemporary music, especially hip-hop. They'd helped throw open the doors that isolated it and brought in light and other sounds to make it the kind of music that would appeal to a wider audience. And, in turn, the music had changed them and spurred them on. They'd always pushed at the boundaries that surrounded hip-hop, and with this release, they were finally down forever. Much as in rock in the late '60s, these days anything went.

OutKast had always taken chances; it was one of the joys of their music. So Big Boi could have his daughter Bamboo on his disc, along with the slow jam "Reset," or the more gospelish "Church" (possibly the first hip-hop gospel piece to reach literally millions of people), and Dre could introduce a wry conversation with God (who happened to be female) about finding the right woman. Unlike *Stankonia*, which was hard and often angry, *Speakerboxxx/The Love Below* was a warm, inviting album that revealed its many joys in repeated listenings; taking it all in during one listen was impossible.

Part of the appeal was its overall soulful vibe. Big Boi's album confirmed family values in their real sense—a commitment to raising his children properly (in his case, that included good schools), while still being a bit of a player. That harked back to what he'd said when *Southernplayalisticadillacmuzik* first came out—that being a player was fine, as long as you took care of business first. And stardom hadn't gone to his head. He still had his priorities very much in order.

Hip-hop certainly remained his first musical love; that much was obvious from the content of *Speakerboxxx*. But he wasn't afraid to experiment with the form and even make fun of it a little, as on the "postlude" to "Bowtie" that closed his disc. On the urgent "Ghetto Musick" he tied together electronic dance music, hip-hop, '80s soul, and the disco-electronic stylings of producers like Giorgio Moroder. It was a track from left field that worked—even though it shouldn't have, given its different elements, all tied together by a Roland 303 line. One of the older tracks, cowritten by Andre, it truly continued the Out-Kast legacy, building on everything they'd achieved before, with a Patti LaBelle sample cropping up to both confuse and delight the ears. It's notable that much of the keyboard work was Andre's—and quite accomplished, too. That same out-there presence was there on "War" and "Church," two other cuts the pair had worked on together. And it was from them you could discern the future of OutKast. "War" was unrepentantly political, a short diatribe against the state of America. Even so, the imposing vision was Big Boi's, and it showed, for those who'd ever wondered, that the band had been a true creative partnership. Andre had been the most visible and often the more verbal, but Big Boi was a vital part of the equation, too—and a major force even when working solo.

Anyone coming in and expecting a record that picked up from *Stankonia* would have found that on *Speakerboxxx*. It wasn't as hard, but there was a continuation of ideas and, to an extent, of sound. One thing there was more of was melody. It popped up continually, in choruses and hooks, pushing the music along and making it all the more memorable.

Given a free rein, Andre, on the other hand, cut completely loose. The most obvious thing was that he moved away from rapping—and hip-hop in general.

"I don't like hip-hop these days," he said, and it was apparent. He'd become disenchanted with the course the music had taken, and his own was leaning hard away. If he seemed to have one real inspiration on *The Love Below* it was Prince, who'd been one of the biggest artists of the '80s and who was still highly respected. Prince, along with Michael Jackson, had been one of the black artists of the period to really cross over and find a huge white audience. Highly prolific and talented on several instruments, he made a good model, largely reinventing and subverting funk with a highly personal vision—not a million miles from Andre himself, in many respects.

You could hear his influence on "Happy Valentine's Day," "Roses," and a few other tracks. And Prince's often explicit sexuality was there in "Spread" and "Where Are My Panties?" (and even in the madness of "Hey Ya!)", which celebrated sex (although the latter also slyly explored the guilt aspect of sex, as opposed to romance). Also, like Prince, Dre was playing guitar and keyboards on the disc, keeping the overall sound more personal.

It was a record where eras mixed and matched, like the '60s blue-eyed soul of "Prototype" where guitar worked against a '90s squelchy bass to strange effect. It wasn't commercial, but it was fascinating. And, as had been Andre's intention when he began writing the soundtrack album, it continued to explore the connections and differences between romance and sex.

"She Lives in My Lap," the original choice for a single,

revolved around a keyboard line that could be as annoying as a bee's buzz. Curiously, it was also one of the songs of his to bring in outside samples, in this case from the Geto Boys and Volume 10, to fill out its sound. It was a piece that teetered on the edge of chaos, held together by the melody of its verses, and an interesting piece of work that demonstrated how far Andre had come as a writer.

As on previous OutKast albums, the interludes were as interesting as the music. From the meanderings of the first disc, they'd gradually developed into pieces with real depth, like the slyness of "God" or the comedy of "Good Day, Good Sir," pieces that served as more than linkage, but stood in their own right.

For someone who didn't think much of his singing voice, Andre used it a lot and performed spectacularly well with it. It was easy to hear, say, Cameo, in the way he sang "Behold a Lady" (and even in the beat behind it)—a real solo track, where he programmed, sang, and played keyboards.

OutKast had never brought in famous cowriters. Instead they'd relied on their own considerable talents. So why had Andre collaborated with R&B star R. Kelly on "Pink & Blue"? Well, he hadn't—the writing credit came from the use of a sample from Kelly's "Age Ain't Nothing but a Number." A tale of love for an older woman that features a luscious chorus, it was once again in the Prince mold, stripped down to a keyboard bass, guitar, and programming—at least until the strings came in. They played a pure, emotive "quiet storm"-style string arrangement, the '80s romantic slow jam style. The string arrangements were one thing Andre couldn't manage. He'd learned a lot about music, but arrangements were still beyond his scope (just about the only thing that was, it seemed).

Strings were also present on "Love in War," the martial beat of which ran counter to its title, while jazz reared its head on "She's Alive," which mixed that style with a Rick James ballad style. If ever anyone needed evidence that Andre had huge commercial instincts, this was it. The odd, elliptical melody sounded abstract alone, but by putting the chorus on top of it, he made it into a fascinating hook for the tale of a single mother—quite possibly his own mother. It was, if you will, a possible sequel to "Toilet Tisha" from *Stankonia*, except in this version the girl stays strong and alive and rears her baby. To take all those elements and make them into a song with a chorus that hooked into the memory was the work of a man whose instincts were sure and whose confidence was very high.

Kelis, of sexy "Milkshake" fame, guested on "Dracula's Wedding," where Andre's mannered vocals were an absolute delight over simple guitar and old school bass. Goofy to the extreme (who else would put a reference to peanut butter and jelly sandwiches into a love song?), it cast old feelings in new fangs. And it was decidedly more accessible than the version of "My Favorite Things," which was possibly beyond the interest of most OutKast fans and was Andre's only real true indulgence on the entire disc. That said, "Take Off Your Cool," the brief, strange duet with Norah Jones, had its odd side and was perhaps unnecessary, although it did give a minor showcase to Dre's acoustic guitar skills on lead and rhythm.

It was hard to hear that "Vibrate" had started life as "She Lives in My Lap," with the multitrack of that cut simply reversed to give the backing. But the bottom line was that it worked, giving a jazzy vibe with muted horns behind the verses and chorus.

The rap of "A Life in the Day of Benjamin Andre" harked back to Andre's teenage days. It was also the most open he'd been about himself and his motivations along with his history, from a girl he'd met in Atlanta to Erykah Badu. While far from a complete tale, it did a least offer some insight—and kept his rap flag flying.

Perhaps the biggest surprise about the double disc was that, operating without editors, there was no filler. Every track hit and hit hard, no matter what style they were attempting.

Although the two discs made a very satisfying package, they still left a lot of questions unanswered. The biggest, of course, was whether Andre and Big Boi would work together again. Inevitably there'd be more OutKast albums, if only because they were contracted to produce more. But whether they'd be solo tracks put together under the group name or not was up in the air. Were the solo albums a sidetrack or the real future?

A few tracks on *Speakerboxxx* gave some indication of where any music they produced together might head, but there was nothing conclusive. And, really, should there be a true Out-Kast album next time around? By then they'd both have moved on anyway and begun investigating new greener pastures of music.

Truth to tell, for all the left-field appeal of Andre's disc, there was little on it that was radically new. He put together some things old and modern, but what he called his "sophistafunk" was fresh only to young ears that hadn't had the chance to hear the different elements before. That familiarity was actually a part of its appeal—it was comfortable and recognizable to older listeners, not threatening in the manner of some hip-hop.

They've become the biggest stars in hip-hop, with only one problem; they're not really in hip-hop anymore. They're in pop music, whether they like it or not. Given Andre's boredom with hip-hop, the next outing could prove interesting for the way their styles might mix more freely than ever before.

For now—and indeed, for the foreseeable future, as there was unlikely to be another new OutKast album before 2005—*Speakerboxxx/The Love Below* was what the public had to make their judgments on.

Andre has said that "every album is a risk. It's not like we make the easiest music to swallow," but this had been a pill that went down easily and brought them to an even higher level, just as each previous release had done. This, though, was of a whole different audience. Its main audience was far removed from hip-hop. It even challenged every perception people had of OutKast, but in the best possible way. They were already in the mainstream; now they were at the front of the pack. And that meant there'd be even greater expectations of them for next time.

To their credit, Andre and Big Boi have never paid much attention to what people wanted from them, always going their own way instead. And they've been lucky that their commercial instincts have meshed with their artistic desires so well.

But the separation is worrying for longtime fans. For the new album they conducted their interviews separately, and the separate sets they performed in concert have to make people wonder if OutKast as a performing and recording entity still exists. For all that, the young men continually deny all reports of a split—and it's worthwhile remembering that those rumors have been going around since 1996 and have proven wrong for many years. The bond of friendship between Big Boi and Andre is very deep and very long.

SPEAKERBOXXX/ THE LOVE
7. BELOW

STRANGE AS it seemed, Big Boi hadn't heard most of Andre's material before he finished the album.

"When I first got Andre's whole record, I must have called him like five times." He laughed. "'Hey, boy! You lost your mind on this one! I'm telling ya!'"

But he loved what he was hearing. They'd heard some of each other's material earlier, as they were both working heavily at Stankonia Studios. Instead of editing each other, one became a cheering section for the other. As Andre put it, "It was almost like being a fan of OutKast," rather than a member. Each could listen from the outside rather than the inside—a weird but pleasant feeling after all the years.

Perhaps surprisingly, there was a narrative to Andre's album, a continuing storyline throughout the whole. It was ostensibly about Possum, an artist type living in Paris who was also a womanizer. He believed he was immune from love—until, of course, he fell in love at first sight, completely and deeply.

Even the title, *The Love Below*, dealt with the inner man, the emotion men can feel but rarely express, which simmers beneath the surface but is never exposed, for fear of seeming less manly.

Andre seemed more anxious about his record than anything, projecting the sense that it was something he had to do, rather than anything he totally enjoyed. It was as if the music was inside and had to come out, but at times he fought against it, rather than letting it flow. And certainly it was a huge departure. In 1994 no one would have guessed that nine years later he'd even be playing saxophone on one of his own tracks ("She Lives in My Lap"). Things had changed beyond recognition.

"My ideas are all across the board now—fashion, painting, everything," Andre said. "I want to put my creative energy into different things. Hip-hop is dead, man. The stuff I do only comes out of the boredom of hip-hop being like it is."

That had been his mantra for a while. He remained the obsessive seeker of the new, wherever it took him, in music or outside it. He'd even begun hinting that he might leave music behind altogether at some point, although taking up new instruments seemed to belie that idea.

Big Boi, on the other hand, seemed to have had a wonderful, easy experience in the studio. Before the album appeared, he acknowledged that "I had so much motherf***in' fun making this record. It's goin' down—I just can't wait till this shit comes out."

Perhaps in some way the idea of two separate albums was a logical move, simply because it was unexpected. OutKast, from the very beginning, had dealt in precisely that, tipping and pushing at the norms until they changed them completely.

For all the image of Big Boi as the regular guy and Andre as the freak, they were both out there, both thoughtful and iconoclastic in their desires and moves. Big Boi had toned down his wardrobe from the time they met back in high school, and Andre had just gone all the way out there.

"He's everchanging and I've changed, too," Big Boi observed. "We've grown at different times, but it's never like we're so far apart that we don't understand each other." But the truthful middle ground, when it came to their music, was in between. They found a place where they could exist—made it, really— and it was well outside the mainstream, which reached a hip-hop peak on *Stankonia*.

"We did something of everything on *Stankonia*," Big Boi agreed. "Any boundaries that were left after *Aquemini*—we blew all that shit away. We felt free to do what we wanted to do." And what they wanted to do was something completely different. There was no going back to the way things had been in 1994.

"There's no way we can get back to the original audience because [back then] we were seventeen years old," noted Andre. "You just can't go back to doing that. That's like trying to relive a childhood. It's just going to continue to grow if people keep movin' on with it." He also gave an indication of his own growth: "When I was young I thought jazz was like something you heard in an elevator. I was never into it. I was never into Hendrix until six or seven years ago. I thought rock music was just noise. But once you get to know it, you think, 'How did he come up with these melodies?'"

He also managed to effectively define the OutKast sound by

saying, "I just make music that I'm not hearing at the time because someone has to do it."

So, ultimately, it was as simple as that; that was what OutKast did. Of course, there was a lot more to it than that. But they did it all simply and effectively—and without a great deal of luxury. Their studio might have boasted top-notch equipment (those were their tools, after all, and they were the workmen), but it wasn't spacious and palatial, luxurious in the manner of some studios. The "live room," where they recorded groups of musicians, was only the size of the average living room, meaning players were cramped and crammed together—not what anyone would expect from a band that had sold millions of albums.

However, that typified OutKast. They could be out there, but when it came to business and money they remained very grounded and practical. They gave interviews and made pronouncements, but more than anything they spoke through the music they made. And unlike so many of their peers, they were eager to step outside the norm and color far outside the lines. That was what made it fun. There could not—and would not—ever be any rehashing of sound for them, whether together or apart.

Artists, real artists, make music for themselves, not to try and sell records. But once a record has been released and sent out into the world, it goes into other hands, with other opinions. Sometimes art and commerce could thrive together—as had been the case throughout OutKast's career—but most often it didn't. *Speakerboxxx/The Love Below* had become one of the most eagerly anticipated discs of 2003, and as soon as it appeared, critics and reviewers were all over it.

In a glowing tribute, *People* called it "the year's most ambitious release" before adding that it was "nothing short of outstanding." Writer Chuck Arnold pointed out that Big Boi's disc was very much in the OutKast tradition, before focusing on Andre's contribution, which he summed up as "the best Prince album that Prince never made."

The *Los Angeles Times* was equally enthusiastic, although the comparisons to Prince were skipped. Together the two discs made a single statement, the writer believed, "that not only cries at the boundaries of rap music but vaults over them" to find a completely new place. It was a new paradigm for hip-hop: "an artistic triumph."

Music magazine *Billboard* even allowed hype to seep through when their review claimed that "this could very well be the year's best album."

Interestingly, *U-Wire* was one of the few reviews to focus on Big Boi's disc, rather than Andre's, summing it up as "more enjoyable," whose "upbeat nature is more fun and the lyrics are much more stimulating." The reviewer also noted insightfully that Andre and Big Boi seemed to have switched their roles of poet and player for this outing: "It's Big Boi who is making political commentary and Dre claiming 'Hey Ya!' is about the failures of monogamy."

For *Interview*, the double set was an examination of hip-hop that was both "incisive and exhilarating," even though much of Andre's disc had absolutely no connection to hip-hop at all, other than his own roots.

A review from the University of Wisconsin called them "simply the best group in hip-hop," which once again sought to put a fence around them that they didn't deserve, while saying the disc "eclipses its genre" indicated that it existed within a single genre—which it didn't.

Perhaps *Keyboard* came closer to reality when they called it "a groundbreaking classic." Certainly, not since the early work of Prince had any music run so rampantly through so many different styles.

It spoke volumes that it had taken almost twenty years for a band to achieve what an individual had done in the mid-'80s. Much of that was a commentary on the music business itself—and the way it pigeonholed music and artists. But it also spoke a great deal about the fact that most artists were happy to settle for commercial, rather than artistic, success. Very few wanted to challenge the norms and upset an apple cart that could promise plenty of wealth.

It was hugely to their credit that OutKast didn't seem to care. And even more so that along the way they'd managed to become massively successful by doing exactly what most people were scared to do.

A big part of that was keeping it interesting to themselves, and that meant pushing further and further. While the reviewers didn't give that much attention to *Speakerboxxx*, it deserved a great deal of focus. Big Boi revved up the OutKast sound on that.

Being political wasn't new, though; they'd done that on both *Aquemini* and *Stankonia*. Nor was the humor, the wordplay, and puns, which had always been a part of the OutKast lyrical magic. But the hyped-up beats and electro-funk was decidedly different, especially for those who'd dismissed Big Boi as the lightweight half of the duo. His album was perhaps more of a revelation than Dre's, inasmuch as it showed him to be the deep thinker of the pair and every bit as musically inventive as his partner, even if he didn't play any instruments. And he was just as capable of writing a catchy song—you only had to listen to the hooks on "The Way You Move" or "Ghetto Musick" to understand that. Where Andre was hyper about whether people would accept the new album, Big Boi's attitude remained as chilled as ever; he knew they'd done good, strong work, and had confidence in his own ears.

Big Boi was really the rock around which the band danced. From the very beginning he'd been a little more understated, content to let Andre take the spotlight—although he could be every bit as witty in interviews.

But there was a deep vein of seriousness under the part of the music he made. "War," for example, was an indictment of politics and war, but from a mature, reasoned perspective, although heavily tinged with anger. "Knowing" looked squarely at America and didn't like what it saw. Big Boi might have moved up from the underclass, but he still understood them completely and agreed with their feelings.

New York magazine seemed to understand that in their review, which called *Speakerboxxx* the "bolder" of the two albums, and suggested that Big Boi "wants to go where most hip-hoppers fear to tread and take the MTV audience along with him," citing the "accessible, democratic nature of its strangeness."

It was necessary for OutKast to maintain a strong connection with hip-hop, even when they'd largely moved beyond it; after all, it was the music that had nurtured them, literally and figuratively. While Andre found little in hip-hop to still interest him, obviously Big Boi did—at least enough to keep him working to change the face of the genre.

OutKast had found a wide audience for their hip-hop that crossed lines of race and gender. They appealed to people who weren't attracted to gangsta rap, with its tough lifestyle and very masculine ideas, where being tougher than the next guy was the order of the day. The street tales had their place, to be sure, but it had reached the stage where they'd become glorifications, and anyone with gangsta credentials and even a partial ability on the mic was landing a record deal (the kind of feeding frenzy that happens when any new style of music gets hot and has been typical of popular music for decades). The emphasis, as with movies, wasn't on verbal and lyrical creativity, but on the violence.

It was music that largely appealed to teenage boys, both urban and suburban. Through it they could have a visceral street life (although it was undoubtedly closer to home for some than others) and take on the toughness of the performers.

While that was more than enough to make huge stars of Eminem, Snoop, and others, and the feuds between rappers helped fuel the ideas of violence (especially following the tragic deaths of Tupac and Notorious B.I.G.), there was little to reach a wider audience.

Over the course of their records, OutKast had completely changed that. They'd subverted the whole thug attitude. Their ghetto streets were the same ones, but the gangstas weren't heroes, just people trying to get by who were going nowhere in the long run. OutKast showed that the streets could bring forth thinkers.

They had before, but the groups who'd come up had never achieved widespread success, partly because they'd always seemed as if they were preaching. No one had connected a conscious vibe with commerciality in quite the same way. And few in hip-hop had been able to come up with hooks and choruses of the same power as OutKast, period.

That was their rare ability, to marry the positive elements with irresistible hooks and fresh thoughts in music. They weren't the first to put funk into hip-hop; it had been around from the beginning with James Brown drum breaks and other elements. They married that with the particular Southern emphasis on bass and brought in ideas from soul all mixed with their own imaginations. That combination was the magic potion, although it was far from a formula.

That had all made their hip-hop into such a big deal. As one writer pointed out, it was hip-hop that could appeal to girls as well as boys. It wasn't threatening or macho, even if they did use some of the language of the streets.

That appeal to females was crucial. They bought a lot of CDs, possibly even more than males, and tended to remain faithful to acts, buying each of their new releases. They were the ones who'd largely propelled acts like Britney Spears, Christina Aguilera, and so many boy bands to multiplatinum status. For a hip-hop group to tap into that market was golden. But the positive aspects of OutKast's music made those who listened to it feel better about themselves, as veteran rapper L. L. Cool J noted: "They've made their fans feel like it's okay to be yourself and given them a feeling of being free." And with the main audience for music of all kinds being teenagers, that was important. They are the years that often bring the greatest conformity, so to reassure people—through music, ideas, and even clothing—that being out of step with the majority was okay offered something different and affirming.

As big stars, both Andre and Big Boi walked a tightrope of celebrity. It would have been easy to fall into the trap of luxury, of having every desire and whim catered to, but they'd managed to avoid that. They didn't appear in the gossip columns with supermodels and movie stars on their arms. Neither was married, but they were both family men. Big Boi was raising his children himself. Jordan was now eight, Bamboo was four, and the youngest, Cross, just three. When he wasn't on the road, that meant he had a handful to deal with—even with help. That was especially true when he also had his kennel business to run. But he wouldn't have it any other way. Like all proud parents, he took part in his kids' activities, going to their soccer games—to the astonishment of other parents, who didn't expect to see someone as famous as him on the sidelines cheering his daughter.

Andre wasn't a full-time parent, of course, but he still made sure he never missed visits with his son. Even when he was rushing to finish work on *The Love Below*, there was no question of canceling a visit by Seven. He even took the time off to take him to Magic Mountain, then had Seven with him in the Hollywood recording studio where he was working. He remembered that his own father hadn't been around and didn't want a repeat of that. No matter if he had other things on his plate, looking after his son and spending time with him was a primary responsibility.

He even began to tone down his wardrobe—at least a little bit—in an attempt to become more of a regular guy (which didn't stop at least a few minor sartorial excesses).

Maybe it had taken him a little longer than his partner, but Andre seemed to be finally growing into himself. After playing the extremes, he appeared to have found more of a middle path that was comfortable. Once the album was complete, he began taking classes in filmmaking at USC in Los Angeles. He was still learning clarinet and saxophone and was particularly proud of the fact that he'd been able to make music on them straight away (the blowing technique for saxophone, the *embouchure*, often needs to be taught before it's possible to get a sound from it). He was learning to arrange music. As one who'd dropped out of high school, then taken his G.E.D. equivalency exam, he was now spreading his academic and intellectual wings wide.

How long it would last remained to be seen, however. By his own admission, Andre has always been a bit of a butterfly.

"I can't be doing something for too long," he said. "My personality leads me to jump into things and learn it. But once I figure it out, it doesn't excite me anymore."

Besides interviews, the pair didn't do a great deal to promote *Speakerboxxx/The Love Below*. There were videos for the two singles, of course, and an appearance on *Saturday Night Live* and the American Music Awards, as well as a few other selected shows, but for the most part they let the music on the disc speak for them. And it was obviously a successful tactic. The record sold like hotcakes from the very first day. To an extent, limiting their appearances was a smart move; it made each one special, with people tuning in simply to see them. Also, "Hey Ya!" and "The Way You Move" were all over radio and MTV, especially the former. It seemed to saturate the airwaves. Not only was it on the pop and hip-hop stations, but almost every format you could find (with the exceptions of jazz, classical, and country). It was a lucky accident of time and place, creating a song so catchy that people heard past the serious message within to find the joy of the music itself and the chorus. It insinuated itself into the brain the way few songs can.

For the last several years the singles market has been slowly declining. Recently that's been due in part to people downloading the tracks they want—often the track that's been chosen as a single, one that they've heard on the radio. But although "Hey Ya!" was certainly downloaded—legally and illegally—hundreds of thousands of times, plenty of people still went out and bought physical copies of it. And the same was true of "The Way You Move." They were simply that huge as songs.

"Hey Ya!" was also a marked departure from the rest of *The Love Below*, with its "sophistifunk." The majority of the album, apart from being sung, had a more relaxed vibe, which was quite deliberate.

"It was soothing to me," Andre explained, "and the music of jazz sounded like where I wanted to be in my life at the time. It sounded real cool and blue." It offered a stark contrast to the urgency of *Stankonia* and also a reflection of how he was changing in himself, becoming less manic and more comfortable with himself.

Between them, Andre and Big Boi covered almost all types of music on this new record, which also helped bring in new fans with the sheer breadth of styles. It was also enough to bring an astonishing six Grammy nominations. That was for Album of the Year, Urban/Alternative Performance, Best Rap Album, Best Music Video, Short Form (for "Hey Ya!), Producer of the Year, and the coveted Record of the Year. They'd also been asked to perform at the ceremony, which would be a major appearance in front of literally millions of people who tuned in for the awards show.

What they'd win remained very much up in the air. There was stiff competition on plenty of fronts, not least from former Destiny's Child leader Beyoncé Knowles, whose solo career had blown up into something huge during 2003, thanks to her massive *Dangerous in Love* album and the chart-topping "Crazy in Love" single she'd recorded with real-life boyfriend Jay-Z that burned up the charts.

It was certain they'd go home with at least something. Rarely did an act receive so many nominations only to walk away empty-handed, especially when their work had been so creative. The fact that they were performing made that even less likely.

Meanwhile, Andre was continuing to check out as much music as possible. He'd become enamored of the new punk and garage bands that were coming out—he even took his DJ to see the Strokes in concert.

"My DJ, y'know, he'd never been to a rock concert before. I don't know if he understood it really." It didn't prove to be the greatest success. "Actually, he fell asleep."

That didn't stop Andre from going to check out other bands like the Hives, the Vines, and the White Stripes. It was very different from the music he was making himself; this was no-frills hard rock, almost primal at times. For someone who was moving toward more laid-back music, it seemed odd, although it did provide the release that only loud rock guitars could.

It also proved Andre was a man of many facets, as many are.

He'd shifted his home out of Atlanta finally, in the wake of his small role in *Hollywood Homicide*. He was eager to do more work in movies, and Los Angeles was the place for that. It was also more of a center for the music business than Atlanta—and perhaps a little more understanding of a teetotal vegan than the South.

Big Boi wasn't about to leave the South, though. His home and business and his life were there. His children attended school there, his family was all there, his roots were in Georgia. Andre was a freer spirit, of the South but not tied to it the way his partner was. For Andre to be too grounded would be to shackle him and his ideas. Big Boi's spirit was nourished by Georgia red clay. His wit, which was a big part of his lyrics, was Southern in its wordplay. His feel for the funk was completely Southern.

The one thing both of them understood and accepted was that the fame couldn't last forever. At some point someone newer—younger—with fresher ideas would come along, and their star would start to slip. But, as Big Boi noted, once you accepted that as a fact of life in the business, "it won't be such a crash." You couldn't plan around it or try to second-guess what people wanted—just to stay in the spotlight a little longer. All you could do was the work that was inside you.

And that was all OutKast had ever done.

For now their career continued to accelerate, but even they admitted that they had no idea exactly where it was headed. They were contracted for three more albums as a band and planned on delivering those. Beyond that . . . well, that was still in the future, and unknowable. But none of those three albums (whatever music was on them) would ever compromise what Dre and Big wanted for themselves. They'd keep pushing at the musical boundaries.

With *Speakerboxxx/The Love Below* selling so well, they were in both the best and worst positions of their career. Best because they'd become literally household names, even with people who had no real knowledge or love of hip-hop. They were going to receive huge amounts of royalties for a long time to come; money would probably not be a worry for either of them as long as they lived, which offered its own freedom. So what could be wrong with that? With the kind of success they'd achieved came the pressure, at least from the outside, to do it again—and *soon.* They were proven hitmakers, and record companies needed those; the more product they could get from them, the better the financial bottom line, which has always been a vital factor in popular music.

OutKast insisted that in spite of the separate albums, they remained a single entity. Perhaps it was inevitable that they would do that, if only because no one wanted to hear otherwise. Most likely it was true. Their musical visions might be different, but there was no reason they couldn't come together; Andre and Big knew each other too well and for too long for that not to be the case. Hip-hop bored Andre, but there was no reason in the world why their next disc had to be all hip-hop. They could exist perfectly well beyond it.

For now they could sit back and enjoy the rewards of their work. While it wasn't the most important thing in the world artistically to sell millions of copies of their album, it was gratifying that people liked it enough to buy it. It vindicated the music.

Not that sitting around suited Andre too much. He seemed to enjoy being busy. Taking film classes and learning new instruments and arranging didn't seem to be enough for him. He'd also agreed to work on Kelis's new disc, helping with the production, and also on the solo album by Gwen Stefani, the lead singer of No Doubt. He'd be joined by Big Boi, and together the two would be producing the work. It was the first time they'd really been outside producers, certainly for a major name, although the surprise was mostly in the fact that they'd never been asked before.

It offered a major challenge, working with someone outside hip-hop—Stefani's background, besides her well-publicized romance with Bush's Gavin Rossdale and her burgeoning fashion career, was in ska and rock (in fact, the closest she'd come to hip-hop was performing with Alicia Keys and Missy Elliott at the 2004 Brit Awards). So it was a test, but a very welcome one. And if it worked, it could elevate the Andre/Big production team to the status of the Neptunes, who seemed to conjure up hit music at will, or the influential Timbaland. It would open plenty of new doors for them and offer unparalleled creativity in a different field.

Andre's new musical knowledge would help, but even he admitted it didn't solve all the problems. He could tell Gwen Stefani how to sing the songs, but he wasn't able to explain the range of notes. He was studying music theory, but he needed to be further along the road to do everything properly. And he wanted to learn. He was thirsty for the knowledge—knowledge of all kinds.

For now, at least, Andre and Big could focus on Gwen Stefani's album, rather than have to think of their own music. They had plans, of course, but plans were always subject to change. The massive sales of their new album had bought them at least a little time and breathing space before the industry pushed down on them again. And to look outside themselves, to work for another artist, was good. It offered a different perspective and would bring in fresh ideas they could eventually use for themselves.

It had been a remarkable ten years for OutKast. In that time they'd gone from being nothing to threatening to sweep the Grammy Awards. And along the way they'd attracted the kind of critical and commercial success (it was rare for the two to combine) that so many bands would kill to achieve.

They'd grown, both in sales and artistically, with every disc. They'd almost reinvented hip-hop, most certainly the definition of the genre, and shaken up music. They'd proclaimed that it was okay to be yourself and not follow trends. And they'd managed to show that responsibility spoke much louder than thuggish behavior. Besides Andre's romance with Erykah Badu, they hadn't been in the gossip columns. They hadn't been arrested. Without even consciously trying, they'd become role models to a generation, as both creators and adults. They'd even managed to shrug off the negativity of the Rosa Parks incident, to move beyond it, even if it wasn't resolved yet.

In short, they were good people who'd been raised right and hadn't forgotten their upbringing. They didn't parade their wealth in a welter of jewelry or flash. They drove good, expensive cars, but their lifestyles weren't extravagant. They continued to morph and grow, but in positive ways. Andre's desire to learn was proof of that, and the way Big Boi's kennel was branching out. They both had real lives outside music, and there seemed to be no appeal for either of them in the celebrity lifestyle.

At the same time, celebrity sought them out. They were a part of popular American culture now, and nothing could show that more than an invitation to appear on *Oprah*, the TV show of Oprah Winfrey, who'd parlayed her own stardom into an empire that included books and magazines. To be asked to appear on her show was an acceptance into mainstream America even greater than the Grammys. It showed that while the music of OutKast was edgy, the people were seen as friendly. They didn't threaten in the same ways as gangstas. They might not be teddy bears—they were both too unpredictable for that—but they didn't threaten at all.

In short, more than any other artists, they'd shown that hip-hop really could grow up and shrug off its ghetto image, that it could be a vibrant, inclusive musical form. They were at the head of the pack.

Andre was right when he said that hip-hop had lost its thrusting direction. It was all too often boring and caught in its own clichés, both lyrical and musical. Unlike so many of their contemporaries, OutKast had never been afraid of humor, whether pointed at themselves or others. Even a put-down like "Roses" was bursting with very dry wit. They also had fun with the music. They loved it, but they didn't treat it with the kind of reverence that others did. It was something to be used to achieve their musical goals. It was malleable; it could be pushed and shoved around. And that was what they did, from "Player's Ball" onward. As they became more confident, they messed with the form more and more, which was how something like "B.O.B.," and the entire *Speakerboxxx/The Love Below* experience could come into being.

With public appearances so few and far between, and Andre adamant that he wasn't going to tour, each time they were performing onscreen had to be something special, and they had extravagant plans for "Hey Ya!" at the *The 2004 Grammy Awards* show.

Mostly, though, they'd be nervous, because of the attention focused on them throughout the show. OutKast and Beyoncé were expected to sweep everything between them, both scooping up fistfuls of trophies. And that was stressful, especially to Andre. When Norah Jones, his duet partner from "Take Off Your Cool," called him the night before the Grammys took place to ask if he was ready, all he could answer was: "I guess I'm as ready as I'll ever be." It was part worry, part resignation.

Maybe the strangest thing was that it even mattered to them. After all, from the start they'd labeled themselves as outsiders, people who didn't need the recognition of the industry as long as their music came out for people to hear. Along the way what was outside had come very much inside. They might have been mavericks, but now they were very much involved with the industry of human happiness. It had happened gradually, but no one was immune, it seemed, no matter where you were, or what you stood for musically. The Grammy stood as the ultimate accolade.

OutKast had been very actively involved in the way their albums were marketed, even offering suggestions of their own and attending meetings. Their rebellion was musical, not social. They might not have liked all the aspects of the music business, but they were savvy enough to know that being inside it and on top of what was happening was the only way to keep control of themselves and their music. Their naïveté about music had worn away very quickly, to be replaced by a very studied awareness. And now they'd climbed close to the very pinnacle. Yes, they'd already won Grammy Awards and been feted, but this time it was all for such a smash hit album that everyone knew—and which had broken so far beyond hip-hop. Whether they liked it or not, they'd become hip-hop's messengers to the mainstream (even if they were no longer a hip-hop band), its ambassadors of a sort to show that hip-hop had fully arrived as part of pop culture America.

That exerted pressure from both sides, really, which wasn't going to make the night any easier for Andre and Big Boi. And although it seemed certain that they would win at least one award, it would have proved very embarrassing, not just for

them, but also for hip-hop in general, if they didn't win anything. Then, on top of all the tension screaming through them,
they had to get onstage to perform—and at least act like they
were loving every second.

THE GRAMMY
8. AWARDS

AT TIMES it seemed as if there couldn't be another level that OutKast could rise to: How much higher could they go? But performing on the *The 2004 Grammy Awards* show in February did lift them up even more. The show, seen on television by so many people (but this time on a five-second tape delay, rather than live, following Janet Jackson's notorious breast-baring incident at the Super Bowl), would broaden their already wide scope. Many of the viewers would be tuning in for the celebrity and pageant, rather than the music itself; almost everyone who listened to commercial radio would have heard "Hey Ya!" and "The Way You Move," but probably a good percentage of the viewers wouldn't have been able to put faces to the members of OutKast or many other groups.

It was also a huge stride forward for hip-hop to have an album nominated for Album of the Year. Eminem's *The Marshall Mathers LP* had been nominated in 2001, but hadn't won, possibly in part because of protests about its lyrical content. And in the 1999 Grammys, Lauryn Hill had taken that category with *The Miseducation of Lauryn Hill* (one of a record-breaking five she won that night), but hers was far more an R&B album, rather than hip-hop. It could be argued that *Speakerboxxx/The Love Below* wasn't really a hip-hop album, but that was how it was perceived by most people—and OutKast was considered a hip-hop band. So for OutKast to win in that category would be a huge advance. After all, rap hadn't even been recognized for a Grammy until 1989.

They were up against a wide range of popular music for Album of the Year: Missy Elliott, Evanescence, Justin Timberlake, and the White Stripes. In contrast, interestingly, all but one of the songs up for Record of the Year had a strong hip-hop influence—Beyoncé, Black Eyed Peas, Justin Timberlake, OutKast, Eminem, and, standing out like a sore thumb, Coldplay, for "Clocks."

It was pleasant weather in Southern California as the guests arrived on February 8 to walk the red carpet into the Staples Center. With 105 Grammy categories to be covered, there was plenty of bustle, and a huge number of people invited. Already, the talk was of the parties after the show that would be provided by the record labels and other companies. These parties tended to be lavish affairs, the places to be seen, where the gossip columnists would gather all the dish to pass on to the world.

The whole business of the awards was meant to generate an

atmosphere of anticipation, climaxing the evening with Album of the Year and Record of the Year awards (in much the same way as the Oscars build up to Film of the Year).

With their six nominations, Dre and Big Boi were in the spotlight all evening; there was simply no avoiding it. They were lucky, however, that Beyoncé walked away with such a handful of awards; suddenly the attention was shifted to her. It meant Out-Kast could relax, at least a little. Not for long, though: The band was up for awards in too many of the big categories. They were up on the stage to receive the award for Best Urban/Alternative Performance for "Hey Ya!," beating out Kelis and "Milkshake" and Dre's ex, Erykah Badu. Then they were back again for Best Rap Album. Not too surprisingly, OutKast lost out in the video category to Johnny Cash's "Hurt," an excellent piece of work, with an award that was also a homage to a legend who'd recently died. Producer of the Year went to the Neptunes instead of OutKast, an understandable result, given their huge successes during the year.

Then it was time for the big awards. When Album of Year went to OutKast, a huge reaction of disbelief/relief crossed the faces of Andre and Big Boi. They hugged each other for what seemed like forever. All the doubts they'd had about releasing two solo albums in a single package were erased. Their accidental masterstroke had paid off big time.

Andre had actually expected the White Stripes to win for *Elephant*. He was a big fan of them and their sound, calling them "the saviors of rock 'n' roll," and given the plaudits they'd been receiving in the press for a couple of years, his expectations were quite justified. Whether he'd have felt cheated if he'd lost to them he didn't say—but in the end it was a moot point. The two of them had done it, boldly planting the flag of hip-hop where it had never gone before.

Record of the Year, though, was a bit more problematic. Coldplay's victory surprised both of them. Andre had expected "Hey Ya!" to win—perfectly reasonable, since it had easily been the most popular single of 2003. Big Boi was even more astonished—not so much because they hadn't won, but because Coldplay had.

Was it sour grapes or was it justified anger? That was a point many could, and would, argue. But the judges had spoken. Coldplay thanked everyone and there was nothing more to be said.

Still, three out of a possible six was hardly paltry. It meant that they now had a total of six Grammy Awards sitting at home, which was hardly shabby; most acts would never collect a single one during their entire careers. It was more proof that they were at the very top of their game.

Andre had thought they'd win three awards on the night; he simply hadn't guessed which categories, beyond Record of the Year, and he'd been wrong on that. It was unfortunate that "Hey Ya!" didn't win, but Andre could take solace from the success of *Speakerboxxx: The Love Below*.

But with the awards came the draining of all the emotion and tension that had been building inside. It *was* a big deal, however much they might have thought it wasn't. And they'd come through intact. Well, almost—there was still the performance of "Hey Ya!" in front of literally millions of people, which provided yet another twist.

OutKast had the prime spot in the show, right at the close, the climax of the entire evening (and tacit acknowledgment, even if they didn't win the award, that they really did have the biggest record of the year). While some viewers might have switched off by then, the majority would still be watching.

Under the circumstances, the kind of performance they could give was limited. It was more about the staging than the music, and OutKast opted for a Native American theme, with a futuristic green teepee issuing smoke as the centerpiece. Andre and Big Boi, both in Indian costumes, were surrounded by dancers who wore feathers in their hair, while a marching band stood behind.

The performance itself was energetic and flawless, with a definite sense of relief and joy. Nothing more than entertainment was at stake, so they could have fun, which they certainly appeared to do.

It was meant as harmless pleasure, and probably no one had given much thought to it beyond having something of a spectacle. But it was about to unleash another firestorm at OutKast, one that made the Rosa Parks debacle look like small potatoes, although hopefully with fewer legal implications.

Having suffered so much adverse publicity from Janet Jackson's Super Bowl "wardrobe malfunction," the network CBS, which aired the Grammys, should have been hypersensitive to anything that could bring criticism. Their five-second delay was meant to take care of any outrageous incidents, but perhaps they hadn't looked too far beyond the surface to think about offending people.

OutKast, too, obviously hadn't considered the whole matter too deeply. It was fun to them, but it was offensive to real Native Americans to see themselves portrayed in such a stereotypical way.

It was only a couple of days before the story was all over the newspapers, as various Native American groups began to lodge protests about the incident. CBS immediately issued an apology, saying they were "very sorry if anyone was offended" by the incident. But a few words weren't about to soothe the waters. Indian groups began to call for a boycott of CBS, and one group even lodged a protest with the Federal Communications Commission.

One of the organizers of the boycott went on record as calling the performance one of the "most disgusting set of racial stereotypes aimed at the American Indians that I have ever seen on TV," while Internet chat rooms filled with anger.

Curiously silent through all this were Andre and Big Boi.

It might not have been too bad if the performance hadn't opened with a real Native American chant.

"It was a Navajo song that I recognized, and I got a little excited," recalled George Toya, a member of the Jemez Pueblo powwow group Black Eagle, who'd attended as winner for best Native American music album for *Flying Free*. He expected to see some authentic Native American music—until the drumbeat changed into the introduction to "Hey Ya!" At that point, "I told my wife, who was sitting beside me, 'Somebody is going to be [angry] about this,'"

The Navajo song was "Beauty Way," and its use upset many members of the Navajo nation.

"To me it wasn't right, especially from the beginning," said Navajo Darlene Yazzie. "They should have had prior permission from the Navajo Nation to use the 'Beauty Way' song. You don't use that kind of song for that kind of performance."

As the drumming continued, actor/singer Jack Black talked over it, before everything dissolved into white noise, and OutKast, along with the dancers, emerged from the teepee.

Navajos object to the context in which their song was used as much as its actual inclusion. Like most traditional Indian songs, it wasn't meant to entertain. It had a real purpose, sung to help restore harmony and balance and as part of the Diné ceremonies.

That was far from the end of the Native American concerns. To many, feathers were a sacred symbol, not to be used as lightly as decoration as they had been on the Grammy broadcast, which they deemed overall to be "racism."

"We're not attacking OutKast as artists," said Native American Cultural Center chairman Andrew Brother Elk. "They can go out and make fools of themselves if they want to, but we are going to question the commercialization of our symbols . . . Our point is: How could no one . . . say, 'This is not entertainment, this is racism?' "

One question no one raised was why a Native American theme had been chosen in the first place. The song had absolutely nothing to do with Native Americans, and there was nothing in its beat to suggest Indians. It seemed an odd choice, as anachronistic as a Western or a kid playing cowboys and Indians.

The Native American Cultural Center even contacted the NAACP, who had OutKast nominated for six awards at their thirty-fifth annual Image Awards ceremony in March, asking the organization to drop the band from its list of nominations.

Throughout the history of the NAACP event, no one had ever been dropped in such a fashion—and among the current nominees was singer R. Kelly, who was facing criminal charges of child pornography at the time.

At *Indianz.com*, a petition was launched. It congratulated OutKast for their awards and achievement, but asked for a full and formal apology for the insults—conscious or unconscious— against the native peoples.

Several people pointed out that if the stereotyping of the performance had been directed at other ethnic groups, it would never have been tolerated—and wouldn't have been televised,

THE GRAMMY AWARDS   161

which was quite probably true. And to date, no one seems to have admitted ultimate responsibility for what happened—whether the concept for the staging came from the band, the network, or from someone else entirely. OutKast and LaFace have stayed silent on the whole affair. In interviews since the awards the incident hasn't been mentioned at all. Although their silence on the issue has not been explained, the incident seemed to die down very quickly after it flared up.

By the time of the thirty-fifth annual NAACP Image Awards it had certainly become a dead issue. Held on March 6, 2004, at the Universal Amphitheater in Universal City, California, it was a celebration of the positivity of African-American society. The biggest winner, perhaps unsurprisingly, was well-loved singer Luther Vandross, who suffered a debilitating stroke in 2003 just before his most recent album, *Dance with My Father*, was released.

Although OutKast were up for a stellar six awards, they ended up with just one, for Best Duo or Group. It was still more recognition, however, which in some ways meant more than a Grammy, because of the ideal for which it stood.

That wasn't the end of the awards ceremonies. The *Soul Train* awards (named for the long-running television show) were set for March 20, 2004. OutKast was not only nominated for R&B/Soul or Rap Album of the Year and the Michael Jackson Award for Best R&B/Soul or Rap Video of the Year, they were also scheduled to appear at the event, held at the Pasadena Civic Center. That night they took home both awards.

It was perhaps just as well that Big Boi was still out in Los Angeles, working on Gwen Stefani's album with Andre, or he'd have needed to do a lot of air commuting during the first few months of 2004. At least he was in L.A. when he wasn't on the road.

Unlike his partner, Big Boi loved to tour. And he not only crisscrossed America, he also took his act overseas, with shows in Europe, where he performed plenty of OutKast material, including "Ms. Jackson" and "B.O.B.," in addition, obviously, to plenty of the songs from *Speakerboxxx*, with "Ghetto Musick" and "The Way You Move" being big crowd-pleasers.

Where OutKast shows had featured live musicians, Big Boi favored just a DJ (DJ Swift, who'd worked on their albums) and four male dancers, although he did bring another rapper, Bubba Sparxx, along with T-Mo from Goodie MOb, and Sleepy Brown, once a member of Organized Noize and now an acclaimed song-writer, producer, and singer in his own right (he was featured on, among other tracks, the single "The Way You Move").

Many of the OutKast hits were in his set, such as "So Fresh, So Clean," but he also detoured into worthwhile obscurities like "Da Art of Storytellin' " for crowds that seemed hungry for Out-Kast in any form, whether whole or halved.

For a few months, unusually, he was the visible one of the pair as he played his shows and relished the traveling life. Andre was keeping his head down on the West Coast, putting time into Gwen Stefani's album and all the other projects he was juggling.

Were they really separating and going their individual ways? Had all the rumors finally been proved correct? Yes—and no. They certainly had separate paths to travel, but that didn't mean OutKast no longer existed— or that it wouldn't in the future. As their own lives developed, with other, more pressing respon-sibilities, they were bound to spend more time apart. But that hardly signaled an end to the band; far from it. There was too much to be gained from working together—and the only way for them to judge just how much was by working apart. Individually they were strong, there was no doubt about that. Together they were unstoppable.

After more than a decade of working so closely with each other, a break had certainly been in order. A group of any kind, whether a duo or more, can become a closed circle. The best way to let fresh air and influences into that was by going outside it, working with others, or even alone, and seeing what happened. They'd literally grown up together, become men together, fathers—it was all a long way from high school dreams and thinking they could do better than the hip-hop they'd seen on television. Perhaps, in their late twenties, it was also time for a little reflection.

One of the problems of being involved in music is that, the more successful you become, the greater the demands placed upon you. It might not be for a fresh album immediately, but there were always other things: sometimes opportunities, sometimes ideas that were worthless. And both Andre and Big Boi were always eager to challenge themselves. Big Boi might not have aspired to be an actor, but he wasn't going to turn down a challenge. And Andre lived to push himself further and further in any and every direction possible.

It was certain, though, that the next thing OutKast did had to be a joint effort. Their time apart had recharged their creative batteries. The world most definitely wanted more from Out-Kast, and the band planned on honoring that. But being completely true to themselves, it might well be something entirely different from what everyone expected—which would be a good thing for both OutKast and their audience. After all, the unexpected was their stock in trade, had been so since the very beginning.

Life had been very good to them, but it wasn't a matter of circumstance. They'd made it through their own hard work, talent, and imagination. They'd never been artificially hyped by a record company like so many other artists. Their work was all their own, not the product of some professional songwriter. They'd developed and followed their own instincts, not afraid of a little controversy, be it musical or lyrical.

Now, a decade on from their first hit, Andre and Big Boi had been able to take the time to catch their breaths. A career in music that lasted that long—and continued to grow—was a rare thing, but they'd managed it, something they'd probably never have predicted when "Player's Ball" first appeared. With ten years down, it was time to start planning ahead for the next twenty.

9. THE FUTURE

Quite where OutKast are going musically is a mystery. Possibly Andre and Big Boi don't even know yet—and won't decide until they start recording beats and ideas for their next album.

We can say with more than reasonable certainty that there will be a next album. Three of them, in fact, because that's what they have left on their contract with Arista, the parent company of LaFace (in a recent company shakeup, L.A. Reid left the presidency of Arista and it's currently consolidating many of its smaller labels; OutKast is currently slated to become part of the Zomba group), and Andre has already said that they're committed to fulfilling their contract.

That's not to say there won't also be solo work, the type of music neither of them thinks falls under the OutKast name. It would, however, have to be music that was quite out there or extremely personal not to warrant OutKast's very broad umbrella, which has managed to take everything from *Stankonia* to *The Love Below* and come out stronger than ever.

Perhaps the biggest shock is Andre's assertion that he might abandon music altogether. Whether that's said to shock or not, it's something he's repeated a few times in recent months. He might abandon hip-hop, but it's unlikely he'll abandon music completely; it's in his blood. Additionally, he's also expressed the desire to attend Juilliard (the best-known music school in the United States) to study classical composition. They might not accept him as a student—after all, he has no background in music, and it's only recently he's learned more of the rudiments—but that would hardly be the action of someone who was completely turning his back on music. He might well be heading into other areas, as indicated by his espoused new love of jazz and his version of "My Favorite Things" on *The Love Below*, areas more removed from the pop vein. But it's unlikely that the idea of creating and expressing himself musically will fall by the wayside.

He certainly understands that anything he does as a solo performer, no matter what the style, will suffer in comparison to OutKast and never be as big. That doesn't bother him (and, in all fairness, he's made ample money from OutKast; commerciality need never again be a factor), as it's about the art, not the sales. So could we see a symphony or chamber work by Andre Benjamin? It's a possibility. Not yet thirty, he has decades ahead of him, and outside pop, most artists do their best work as they grow older. That he has talent isn't even a question. Where it takes him certainly is. He'd struggle to be taken seriously in jazz or classical music, arriving at it so late. But it's not impossible that he could find a home there.

Abandoning music certainly hasn't occurred to Big Boi. At present he's largely been the one carrying the OutKast flag on his tour. But he also has solo plans that extend beyond the band. He's been working on a solo album—completely solo this time, without Andre's involvement at all—under the assumed name of Hot Tub Tony, which might reveal more of his R&B side, in the style of the late Barry White, whose slow jams were made for romance and sex. Additionally, he and former Organized Noize member Sleepy Brown have started an as-yet unnamed group. He won't just be sitting back and waiting for the royalty checks to arrive.

One thing that's said to be in the OutKast musical works is another compilation, this time celebrating ten years of the band. It will, however, be a little late for the anniversary—for almost any anniversary, really. Given the fact that Andre and Big Boi first teamed up in 1990 and that the initial release of "Player's Ball" came just prior to Christmas 1993, the decade has come and gone. Even their first album, *Southernplayalisticadillacmuzik*, arrived in April 1994.

And what might be on there that hadn't been on *Big Boi and Dre Present . . . OutKast?* A selection of studio outtakes, different mixes, and possibly unreleased material would be what fans wanted. They've had ample chance to catch up with the band's back catalogue, so they'd need some surprises and rarities to make it all worthwhile. Obviously, any new collection would also need the major tracks from *Speakerboxxx/The Love Below*—which would, in fact, be the hook for those few who hadn't already bought it.

It would be a shame if the collection proved to be exploita-tive, as so many similar compilations are. A best-of once in a de-cade made sense; to appear more often a band would need hit after hit or an intelligent selection of material. And OutKast was capable of providing the latter. There were a number of completed tracks that had never been released, for several rea-sons: the band may not have liked them or maybe they didn't fit in the general pattern of an album. There was even the possibil-ity of OutKast creating something entirely new for such a release, too, as they had with "The Whole World" just a few years earlier.

Other than being artists, their careers as outside producers were just beginning. Be it together or alone, they'd proven themselves to be very strong in the control booth. Working on Gwen Stefani's album was probably just a beginning, especially if it does well. Of course, what they could do for others paled in comparison to what they could do for themselves, where they could take every kind of chance, but they brought a left-field sensibility to everything, and a commercial track record that spoke for itself. Pop acts had been seeking out hip-hop and R&B producers for several years now; there was no reason OutKast couldn't fill out their calendars with studio work in the future. In all likelihood, though, it would never be more than a second-ary string to their bow, and they'd be very selective about the acts with whom they worked.

First and foremost on their agenda, however, was another video. Working with longtime video collaborator Bryan Barber, they were shooting a clip for "Roses," which had been picked as the next single. Given its language, it was unlikely to receive widespread airplay (especially in the cleanup of the airwaves that had followed the Janet Jackson Super Bowl incident). Like several of OutKast's videos, there was a story of a sort to it—in this case, a kind of reenactment of the musical *West Side Story* (which, in itself, was a modern retelling of Shakespeare's *Romeo and Juliet*).

It was about a rivalry between two high school gangs, Andre explained. "We're pretty much after the same girl, Caroline, and she's in a girl group called Roses, with pink jackets."

Andre and Big Boi would portray the leaders of the two gangs, both performing onstage to win Caroline's heart. Members of Goodie MOb, plus former P. Diddy valet Farnsworth Bentley (now, it seems, a celebrity in his own right) were also making cameos in the piece.

It could be seen as a warm-up for their next major project, which was also going to be on the screen, rather than in the recording studio. Before that, they did take time to induct Prince into the Rock and Roll Hall of Fame on March 15. It was an apt pairing, given Prince's influence on a young Andre—an influence still apparent on several tracks of *The Love Below*, especially the new single!

Then, finally, they could start to focus on the film. Currently without a title, the impetus probably came from Andre, who'd been eager to be involved in the business. He wanted to be a part of the process from inception to completion. He'd even worked on the script, "kicking around creating stories with a couple of partners I know." And he planned on spending a lot of time on the set, learning how to direct a film—which was another of his many ambitions.

The film was being made for television cable channel HBO, and was set, surprisingly, in the 1930s Prohibition era—a far cry from the modern world OutKast inhabited. With a strong starring cast, including actors Don Cheadle and Rosario Dawson, it wasn't being done on a tiny budget; this was no vanity project.

Big Boi admitted it was "gonna be different as hell for us," but insisted "it's gonna have that special OutKast touch, just on film."

Of course, there would be a soundtrack album, and that was already penciled in as the next OutKast release. Exactly what type of music it might contain—modern? period?—no one was saying, if anyone even knew yet.

Unlike music, which they knew all too well by now, film was going to be sink or swim for them with a very steep learning curve. And even more than music, it was an unforgiving arena. The amounts at stake were much higher, and there was even less forgiveness of failure. OutKast was a big name in music, but in film they meant nothing—and certainly not in a film set in the 1930s (a hip-hop film might well have been different).

But it was typical of Andre to dive into something completely. He'd enjoyed his role in *Be Cool*, playing a rapper named Dabu. He already had another role lined up, this one much bigger, playing guitar icon Jimi Hendrix, who lit up the '60s with his electrifying wizardry. The movie was set to be directed by the Hughes Brothers (who'd made *Menace II Society*, among other movies).

"When the Hughes Brothers asked me to consider a role as Jimi Hendrix, I was honored and thought, 'Hey, I'd love to do that.' Right now we're in negotiations with the Hendrix estate to get the rights to make the movie, so I have no firm idea when the film may start, but it could be as soon as this summer."

On that project, Andre said with confidence that he wouldn't even attempt to play Hendrix's guitar parts. Although he played the guitar, Andre knew he wasn't in the same class as one of the modern geniuses of the instrument. Andre decided to leave the playing up to a professional guitarist, who could at least imitate the master. With his psychedelic, colorful style, and his spectacular Afro, Andre was a natural for the role. He looked the part, even down to his often-outlandish clothes, and the wispy goatee.

He loved trying new things, and this would be something major for him, a film role he could really sink his teeth into, something that would make or break him as an actor. Hendrix's popularity and legend had grown in the more than three decades since his death, and his influence was still huge. That meant the film would be high profile, and with it, Andre's portrayal of the man would be scrutinized very closely. If he did well in the part, his future as a screen actor (and he'd made no mention of trying to conquer live theater, only movies) was assured. If he bombed, then he could probably kiss any other large roles good-bye forever.

Maybe he didn't really care too much about an ongoing acting career, though. He'd also mentioned attending college, particularly Oxford in England, one of the world's most storied universities. It was home to an intellectual elite—only the very best were given the chance to study there, which perhaps made it an odd, and ambitious, choice for someone who'd dropped out of high school and graduated with a G.E.D. But people develop at different paces. His thirst for knowledge was obvious. Maybe he wouldn't be accepted at Oxford, but he would be somewhere—if he really wanted. And all of it was okay with Big Boi.

"He wants to go to Europe or do movies, I'm fine with it," he stated. "Our love for each other is greater than our love for music."

And it was. They were still the best of friends, tied tighter than ever now that they were adults, godfathers to each other's kids. Although they saw less of each other these days, the bond was stronger than ever. It was difficult to imagine things might ever be any other way, for as long as they both lived.

In a couple of interviews, Big Boi had said that OutKast had plenty of material already in the vaults for their new work—enough for about six albums, he claimed. And they'd already worked out what was going where. After the soundtrack, the second album was the one he was "totally waiting for. There's going to be a lot of rapping on that motherf**ker from both of us."

They'd always been ahead of the curve, but this seemed like a dangerous strategy. The world of music could move fast—if someone came along with something very fresh and different. If they did release material that had been recorded a couple of years earlier, it (at least) was a gamble; it could easily be out of date by the time it reached the market—and certainly not representative of where OutKast currently stood.

But Andre hinted that they might not be relying on old unreleased songs when he discussed their contract with Arista. He admitted that it was "actually financial decisions to record these albums, and that's on the real." It was the use of the word "record" that was interesting, suggesting that they hadn't been made yet.

So a great deal remains to be seen. OutKast is by no means over yet, and the release of three albums, especially if two of them still have to be written and recorded, will take quite a while. More and more, Andre and Big Boi have become perfectionists in the studio. They know what they want and they've learned how to achieve it.

So far, OutKast has been about the long journey from teenagers to men—and becoming comfortable with that. They've thoughtfully raised issues which occur to all men, not just those within the black community—how to look at war, relationships, fatherhood—as well as racial concerns, like "Rosa Parks." When the world of hip-hop seemed to be sliding down some violent streets, they kept their sensibilities.

There's no doubt that there's a crossroads ahead—three albums distant. Until that time, their future is assured by a contract. And they don't even have the same freedom they did when they were younger, with just a couple of hits to their credit. OutKast is big business these days. That means the standards and expectations have increased. Effectively, by selling so many records, they've fenced themselves in a little bit. They might not have quite the same freedom to creatively roam at will that they once enjoyed. To sell less than six million copies of their next album (the same figure which *Stankonia* eventually managed) would be seen as a failure in the light of *Speakerboxxx/The Love Below*, which passed that magical diamond (10 million) mark in the summer of 2004. And, ultimately, the record label has control over what's released.

Andre's jaded with hip-hop, but it's certain he'll put his heart and soul into any new work; that's simply the way he's always been. It might be a convoluted journey, but it's always a passionate one.

It's interesting, too, that Andre has begun his own line of clothing, separate from the OutKast brand. Going under the name of Benjamin Andre (a pseudonym he's been using more these days—it even crops up in the title of one cut on *The Love Below*), he's begun with accessories, rather than the standard jeans and T-shirts that have been the staple of so many labels, including OutKast's own. From socks to handkerchiefs, it's aimed at men, helping them achieve that total look.

According to all reports, however, the OutKast clothing brand continues, and there are no plans for it to cease operation; in fact, it's largely run by Big Boi these days. Along with FUBU, Sean John, and ROCAWEAR, it remains a staple and popular at many outlets, having become a very successful business in casual clothing. Andre's new line is more upmarket, and certainly less casual, but if he can find a niche among the fashion-conscious, he might do well. Additionally, he also had a line of children's clothing in the works—a perfectly understandable move for a parent.

That changes are going on within OutKast are undeniable. The production on *Speakerboxxx/The Love Below* wasn't credited to the Earthtone III company Andre and Big Boi had started several years ago. In fact, that company no longer exists. Instead, they each have their own production companies—in Andre's case, it might be concluded that his includes the development of movie properties.

Inevitably, this separation continues to fuel rumors that Out-Kast no longer exists as an entity, no matter how much Andre and Big Boi say otherwise. But they've been working together on Gwen Stefani's album and also on the upcoming movie. Whatever moves are made in business don't necessarily reflect on art and friendship. As long as they have something to say together, OutKast will exist. There's been no falling out among friends.

At the same time, the rumors have been understandable.

Groups do disband, people grow apart, their interests and ambitions change. A lot depends on how secure the people involved are within themselves. And both Big Boi and Andre have proved themselves to be mature, secure individuals, both highly driven and motivated to succeed at whatever they do—and their track record so far hasn't shown any failures.

Work remains very much at the center of Andre's life. Learning and trying new things keeps him going. An only child, he's always been able to be self-reliant. The only serious relationship he's had was with Erykah Badu, and in its wake he's frequently questioned the nature of human and romantic relationships, wondering whether people are supposed to be monogamous. Quite notably, Andre hasn't pursued any deep relationships since Erykah, whether high profile or otherwise. In that way he's been something of an emotional drifter, but willing to make his art one of the centers of his world.

He has, however, maintained an excellent, involved relationship with his son. Being a parent who doesn't see his child all the time has naturally made things more difficult—each time he has to get to know a bit of Seven afresh—but still immensely satisfying. And he's made the time to be with his son. That he'll continue to do so is unquestionable. Seven is his responsibility, and he'll live up to all his responsibilities, not only in name but in deed, until his son becomes a man in his own right.

Andre is a busy man; that much is quite obvious. But he makes time for Seven, even taking him to the set of an OutKast video once. He's learned to combine business and pleasure—although he's learning that a growing boy can also be a lot of work and take a lot of energy, especially when you don't see him on a daily basis. And Andre will continue to make the time even as he gets busier.

He's talked so often recently about quitting the music business that it's become like the boy who cried wolf—if it ever really does happen, no one will quite believe it. But he certainly does continue to focus on acting, with yet another movie in the works, an independent feature called *Love Hater* ("The director liked my song so much, he renamed the movie after it"—an echo of *The Love Below*, although you have to hope for his sake that it doesn't meet the same fate), where he'd be playing the lead character, opposite Hawaiian-born actress Shannyn Sossamon (*A Knight's Tale, The Rules of Attraction*). Again, there was no word on when shooting was likely to begin, but it would have to be arranged around the rest of Andre's rapidly filling schedule.

It probably wasn't happening deliberately, but between his own music, movies, producing, and clothing lines, he was building quite a little empire around himself. It wasn't IBM, but there was still plenty of money involved, and he knew he had to stay on top of it all because, as he said, "This may not last forever."

His lifestyle isn't especially extravagant. He eats at good restaurants where he can find vegan fare, has property, both for himself and as investments (managed by his mother), but he isn't the type to be seen at each and every party or on the club scene. Often he simply prefers his own company rather than having people around him. And with all his commitments, be they business or family, that kind of time is becoming harder and harder to find—and more and more precious.

Realistically, the idea of taking time off to go to college is out of the question, at least in the next few years. He simply doesn't have that kind of free time, short of walking away from everything he's built. And while that isn't impossible, it is highly unlikely. But, down the line, who knows? He was half of Out-Kast, and they'd always provided the unexpected.

"Right," he agreed. "It's like, what the hell would an Out-Kast fan not expect?" For now, though, he feels like he is on a mission of some kind. He just doesn't know yet exactly what it is. "I have no idea. But I know I'm not finished just yet."

Andre is the only one who seems to be cut out for bigger things. Big Boi also has a plate full of work in front of him. He is limiting himself to music, though, and seems quite content with that. There's his work with Janet Jackson on some tracks for a new album, as she sought a new sound to return her from relative obscurity, plus producing tracks for Tennessee rappers 8Ball and MJG. Then there is his solo work, and touring, which helps to fill up the time very well.

Music, particularly hip-hop, still obviously moves him in a way it no longer touches his partner. And he, too, is on a mission: to raise the level of hip-hop away from guns, money, and drugs. Big Boi's already proved himself to be one of the wittiest rappers around, able to twist and turn lines very skillfully.

Now he wants others to follow his example, to make hip-hop into a more positive force. There are already acts like Common or The Roots who are doing that—and both of those use soul and even some world music as part of their lexicon—but there are very few acts in the bestselling mainstream who've shown any inclination toward it. Instead they give the people what the people seem to want—more bling-bling for their buck.

After ten years of working with Andre, Big Boi understands the need for some separation—and feels it himself.

"We just both kind of getting older, finding new interests and new things that excite us in different ways," he explained. It is a perfectly natural thing, and for him, too, it isn't going to affect the "brotherhood" he feels with Andre.

He also has his other real interest: the Pitfall Kennels. That continues to thrive—in fact, business has been booming since the ad appeared in the CD booklet for *Speakerboxxx/The Love Below*. His contact with it isn't daily, but it remains his venture, and he is involved in decisions that have to be made about the dogs and about breeding. From starting out with nothing, and knowledge gleaned from books, he's made it into a thriving, respected concern with its own breed, which is every bit as big an achievement as Andre getting into movies.

And he has his three children, who've remained quite firmly in the center of his world. He dotes on them and probably spoils them a little, too. Just like Andre, he takes his responsibilities as a parent very seriously, and he is also the primary caregiver for them all. That means taking care of the little as well as the big things: going to soccer games, taking them to the mall and to school. It isn't glamorous, but real life for most people doesn't include rubbing shoulders with stars. Big Boi has plenty of time for that. The nitty-gritty of daily life helps to keep him very much grounded in reality. Unlike a lot of celebrities who live their lives in a cocoon, Big Boi knows the price of a gallon of milk.

But Big Boi still likes living up to his image as a player sometimes: Why else does he have a stripper's pole in his basement (the one he showed to MTV when they filmed an episode of *Cribs* at his house)? But with three kids in the house these days, it probably gets very little use. There is usually a big gap between image and reality.

He seems comfortable with living in a relatively small town, and unlike Andre, there is little danger of him relocating out of the South, or even out of Georgia. He is proud of his roots there, and the pace of life suits him. His family and his work are there. He certainly doesn't need to seek bigger opportunities; they come looking for him these days—the chance to work with so-and-so or produce so-and-so. Also, he had his road time, his release of fun and responsibility when all he had to do was show up and deliver the goods onstage.

Touring was a strange life, wonderful for those who enjoyed it, pure torture for those who didn't. It could be eerily like the movie *Groundhog Day*: living the same day over and over with slightly different scenery, or an adventure. Andre saw it as the former, Big Boi as the latter, a chance to get out and see the country—or countries, depending where he was headed.

As any single parent could testify, a break from looking after three kids—even with help—is almost always welcome. Wonderful as they are, almost everyone needs a break from kids at times, a chance to hang out solely with adults.

Unlike Andre, it's very doubtful that Big Boi has ever seriously considered quitting music. And certainly not for a career in film; he's shown no inclination to become a screen presence. The only place he wants to step out is on record or onstage. He still sees hip-hop as a way forward, certainly for himself, and it's his music of choice, although he still listens as widely as he ever did. And he still harbors a desire to work with one of his teenage inspirations, Kate Bush. Given that she's reportedly been back in the studio working on a new album, her first since 1993's *The Red Shoes* (released, notably, before OutKast's own recording career even began), it's not completely out of the realm of possibility, although it's probably still quite unlikely.

While he loves hip-hop, that doesn't mean he's happy with the state of it—which is why he's tried to change it, to inject the humor back into it, and bring some positivity to the party. And, given the immense success of OutKast, it may just be a matter of a short time before others follow his lead.

And Big Boi helped put the funk back into hip-hop, when it seemed it had lost its way musically. One listen to *Speakerboxxx* makes it apparent that his contribution to the duo was every bit as great as Andre's; in fact, he's the foundation that allowed Andre to fly so high and so far. He loves bass, and on *Speakerboxxx* alone came up with some inspirational beats. But he could also appreciate what Andre achieved with *The Love Below*. The two CDs function as two halves of a single whole—that's why it can ultimately work as an OutKast album as effectively as any of their previous releases.

He might play the straight man to Andre's visual freak, wearing athletic clothes or dressed up (but not the extreme ghetto fabulous of his partner), but don't be fooled. Go below the surface and there's a man who doesn't subscribe to any of the conventions—and never has. That's why OutKast are OutKast. Both of them have always been outsiders, and surface appearances are deceptive. In his own way, Big Boi is further out there than Andre. Where Andre has pushed back the boundaries, Big Boi has been happy to subvert hip-hop from the inside, and that's not easy. He deserves far more credit than he's been given, and possibly in another decade, when there's some more distance, he'll finally receive it.

It will be very interesting to see where he goes with his own music in the future. The solo project under the name of Hot Tub Tony could see him taking a completely different direction, quite possibly toward soul, while the band with Sleepy Brown also contains interesting possibilities.

He seems less concerned with the future than Andre, and overall less subject to ups and downs, and insecurities about whether listeners will like new material. He simply writes and performs it, then sends it on its way to stores and radio. Perhaps that's a healthier attitude overall, simply creating and letting business take care of the rest. But it fits in with Big Boi's laid-back Southern demeanor and sense of humor. Whatever happens, will happen. He takes care of his part, of all that he can, to the best of his ability, then lets others take over.

So far his instincts have been unerringly on the mark. They may not always be that way, as he grows older and the music changes behind him, but that's almost inevitable for any artist. If he does reach the point of retirement, it will certainly be with good grace and gratitude for the run he's had. And with his money, his investments, and his thriving kennel, he won't be going away empty-handed. Like Andre, he won't ever want for anything again, and probably neither will his children.

Speakerboxxx/The Love Below did a huge favor for both Andre and Big Boi. As well as being their biggest-selling album by far as OutKast, putting them front and center on the musical map, it also firmly established them as individuals. For the future that is vital.

That they'll have solo careers is inevitable—they've both

made that quite apparent. And there's no reason they shouldn't, although the musical range of OutKast is so wide that it could probably accommodate almost anything. But in the wake of this disc, they're both separately known and recognized now. It may well be that whatever they do alone won't be as big as the work they do together—they're known apart, but OutKast these days is virtually a brand—but it will be heard, and will sell, in whatever quantities.

While not a deliberate career move, it's worked very neatly. And with a perfect naturalness, they've also been able to establish their different personalities, with Andre as the off-the-wall bohemian, the vegetarian in loud, strange clothes whose music often produces the unexpected, the wild card. Big Boi is the proverbial sharp-dressed man, the player who takes care of business, the one who can take on the thugs on their own territory but makes everything positive. They're the unlikely opposites who've attracted for so long, but each is able to stand strong on his own as well as together.

That's also a powerful commercial combination, as they've proved time and again over ten years. It's also been a pile-driving artistic force, one that's changed the face of hip-hop, bringing it to the masses, and also indirectly influencing black pop music as a whole. Much of the so-called neo-soul movement has sprung up in the wake of OutKast's early success, fusing soul, funk, and hip-hop into one package. They were years ahead of the Neptunes in using a falsetto, Curtis Mayfield-type voice to sing the hooks in their songs. Much as the Beatles's influence over pop as a whole lingered for years, it's quite possible that acts will be mining the seams opened up (but largely unexplored in detail) by OutKast for a decade or more. There are plenty of nuggets in there, waiting to be polished and examined.

They proved that you can be both different and successful, and that formula is a shackle more than a guide. Certainly in their wake, black pop (if not hip-hop) has enjoyed the kind of glory days it hasn't seen since the 1960s or early '70s, with an acknowledgment and celebration of its roots combined with a sometimes radical sense of adventure. How much of that can be attributed to OutKast will probably never be known, but the coincidence in timing is definitely intriguing. Even if they weren't a direct inspiration for the sound, their success must have acted as a catalyst for both looking back and looking ahead. And to change the face of music is a massive achievement.

Actually, to even have a ten-year history in music today is remarkable. It speaks of a tremendous longevity and energy. Listen to their albums in order, and the growth, in every possible way, is self-evident. From their first album, where they were trying hard, but still sounding imitative in their flow and style—but still giving it plenty of funk, thanks to Organized Noize—all the way through to *Stankonia* and *Speakerboxxx/The Love Below*, which glow with all the confidence of people at the very top of their game, willing and eager to take chances—and doing it almost routinely.

Each disc builds on what went before, using it as a step to climb higher. You can almost chart the progress, and the way they've looked outside themselves for lyrical inspiration (as well as keeping a gaze within, and not being afraid to criticize themselves or apologize, as on "Ms. Jackson").

Each disc has also marked them taking on more and more

responsibility. Beginning with *ATLiens*, they began making more of the beats and the music, and used live musicians, as opposed to everything programmed, setting themselves apart from the hip-hop mainstream (that had also been evident on their debut). But real funk needs live players and human interaction.

Buying their own studio gave them total control over the creative process. Of course, everything still has to be approved by the record company before it's released, but owning a studio gives complete freedom to come and go and experiment at will. And the leap from *Aquemini* to *Stankonia* showed they'd used their time wisely. The former might have been a widely lauded album, but the latter was a quantum creative leap into the stratosphere.

With *ATLiens* and even on *Aquemini* they were young and brash enough to let their excesses show. By *Stankonia* they hadn't so much tamed those excesses as learned how to use them properly—and to their own advantage.

They've kept moving forward. Individual tracks on albums might take strange turns, but there really has been a relatively straight path in their music. It wasn't apparent at the time, of course, but in retrospect it becomes clearer.

Most likely, even when their first album came out and sold well, they couldn't have imagined their lives as they are today. They might have dreamed of long-term success, as anyone involved with music would, but to be able to go the distance is another matter entirely. And to spin that off into a clothing brand has been even better.

And along the way they've become as rich as they could ever have dreamed. While it was never a goal in itself, it's certainly been a very happy by-product. It's given them freedom to pur-

sue other things and to create real, long-term futures for themselves and their families. For anyone to achieve financial security
is an achievement, and they've managed it before the age of
thirty. Small or large, they can now try anything they desire
without worrying too much.

CONCLUSION

THERE ARE still plenty of people who believe that OutKast no longer exists. But even though Andre stated that "In a perfect world, this would be the last OutKast record" (meaning that they'd leave on a high note), that's simply not the case. The movie and its soundtrack attest to that.

Yet that doesn't mean it'll function in the same way it had before. They've turned down plenty of opportunities lately, including a Tennessee festival, which would have earned them a million dollars for a one-hour set. They've been asked to do ads endorsing several different products and refused them all. And, of course, Andre's refusal to tour has meant a lot less income.

Obviously, that's been frustrating to Big Boi, although Andre seems perfectly content with his position on the matter. While

Andre lives his dreams, like starting a rock group fronted by
Johnny Vulture, the guitarist he played in the "Hey Ya!" video,
Big Boi remains "the Jesse Jackson on the group—'Keep hope
alive.'"

It's a delicate balancing act between the two, but that hardly
means it's over. Dre is less committed and less focused on Out-
Kast than he once was. Having succeeded beyond a level most
people could never even imagine, there's little left for him to
dream for with OutKast. How much more can they achieve?

That remains to be seen. With one album planned after the
soundtrack, its whole concept and title already in place—and
note that it's an album with a concept, not just a collection of
tracks, meaning it will be new recordings—the future does
remain open. Andre might talk and do other things, but he
hasn't completely turned his back on the band. He's confessed
that "I get bored really fast" (which is another reason he hasn't
been able to settle into another romantic relationship, along
with the fact that he's noticed an artist's work suffers when
he's happy; it happened to him when he was with Erykah),
although that's hardly a revelation. If he was content to stay in
the same place, a lot of OutKast's music might never have happened.

There's nothing to stop him spreading his wings wider and
still be half of the band. His love of jazz is growing, and he'll
certainly investigate that more, possibly in the slightly tweaked
manner of "My Favorite Things" from *The Love Below*. He's
become an adequate guitarist who loves garage rock. Maybe
he'll release solo albums in both those fields, knowing that what
he has to prove is artistic, not commercial.

He's on a journey, and where it will take him, nobody knows—
not even Andre himself. But it's fitting that the kid who was a

skateboarder when everyone else was hanging out in the projects should go his own way, even if it's far from the pack. He has reportedly lost interest in both the OutKast clothing line (concentrating instead now on his Benjamin Andre line) and the Aquemini record label, both of which are looked after these days by Big Boi.

It is safe to say that he won't still be rapping in another ten years, though. He's certain of that, and it's easy to believe him when he insists that "rap is about youth and energy." And he has no wish to spend his life on a nostalgia trip, reliving old hits for aging crowds.

That doesn't mean he's right. There's no hard and fast rule that rap is for the young, and maybe Big Boi will be the one to prove him wrong. He's developed his skills, and he's not going to let them go to waste when he's completely on top of the game.

Maybe they will go their separate ways once they've fulfilled their contract, and OutKast will become a thing of the past. That happens all the time. Bands break up and move on. By the time it does, though, they'll have had a huge run.

Possibly nothing else they create will have the incredible success of "Hey Ya!" After all, that's the kind of once-in-a-lifetime song that's a gift. And one given very rarely. So realistically, everything will pale in comparison to that. However, that's fine. They'll certainly still sell plenty more records. And it's not as if they need the money from performances, endorsements, or even more record sales—they're both very comfortably set for life.

More than anything, the problem is one of security—and even that might be imagined. Big Boi likes the security of Out-Kast, of the name, the history, and working with his closest friend. He feels comfortable with that, although he's proved himself more than capable of working alone and with others. Andre 3000, on the other hand, has come to see OutKast as limiting, although he's proved time and again that it's not. Instead, the pair of them have made OutKast into the kind of liberation they originally intended when they came up with the name. It's flexible, malleable, and able to contain anything they want to put in it. What OutKast is—and what it becomes—is determined by only two people: Andre and Big Boi. CD buyers might have their own ideas, but they're not the ones in control. A record label might refuse tracks (although, at this point, the music would have to be very weird indeed for them to do that), but only Dre and Big can determine what happens under the OutKast name.

It's perfectly possible that Andre will change tack again and decide to really pursue the possibilities of the band, while investigating other music on the side. It could happen quite easily that something triggers his enthusiasm again, that some left turn in hip-hop excites him and brings him back into the fold or that something he and Big Boi do on one of their next two albums pushes hip-hop even further. In other words, nothing is written in stone.

There's a curious irony in the fact that while OutKast has hardly performed in support of *Speakerboxxx/The Love Below*, it still feels as though they've been overexposed recently. Even into 2004 they've been on the covers of many magazines, following their Grammy success (in fact, they've received more print coverage for their three Grammy wins than Beyoncé did for her five!). Their videos were everywhere.

Normally, album sales should have tailed off six months after release. But, thanks to those Grammy Awards, *Speakerboxxx/The Love Below* continues to be a hot property. Not the way it was for the final three months of 2003, but still moving at a very generous rate. It simply wouldn't go away, reaching that magical diamond plateau in the summer of 2004.

Success breeds success, as this has certainly shown. And it'll prime the pump for the movie, its soundtrack, and the album that arrives after. Big Boi has shown his willingness to bend and compromise on the movie, and Andre has on the disc that will come later. As long as they continue to do that—and with a deep, lasting friendship at the core, they should be able to manage that—then OutKast will continue.

It's been an odd trip so far, from red clay Atlanta basements to movies and topping charts all over the globe, but one neither of them would have missed. So many people say they can do better than the videos they see on television or the music they hear on the radio, but so few ever do anything, let alone prove themselves right. From the very beginning OutKast has had an individual vision, even if it initially needed to be taken in hand and edited by others. They've also been lucky, in that they've always been given the chance to experiment a little, to let their imaginations run riot, rather than being pushed to retread the clichés of hip-hop.

Ultimately, it's about opportunity, talent, and imagination. The last two OutKast has possessed in abundance, and they haven't shied away from using them. As they've grown, so have their imaginations, until they now seem positively boundless.

They've also been lucky to have had the opportunity to release albums. LaFace believed in them and didn't try to force them in any particular direction, believing instead in what they had to offer. There are many more talented rappers than there are albums. Promotion and radio play have both helped, but it should be remembered that their initial break came through word of mouth, when "Player's Ball" became the soundtrack to

Freaknik week and a staple in the Atlanta clubs, a challenge to all the New York DJs who dominated the scene at the time.

They've always represented the South and still do, although Andre's vision has certainly become more cosmopolitan, and they're as likely to be seen in New York, L.A., or even at a fashion week in Milan, Italy, as they are on Peachtree Street in Atlanta these days. They've kept the booty-shaking bass in their sound, a reminder of home, of their roots. Their fans are wide-ranging. Even artists like Dave Matthews and Pink love their music—and understand their influence.

"We came in the door as a hip-hop group, but it's exceeded hip-hop," said Big Boi. "We are hip-hop, reggae, jazz, blues, soul, funk, everything."

They're the history of music in one bright package. And in the past also lies the future. It's difficult to be original when you're not intimately familiar with what's gone before, and originality—at the very least a mix-and-match selection—has always been OutKast's long suit. It's impossible to imagine them ever repeating themselves.

Andre is OutKast's wandering spirit, and Big Boi is its heart. Together they'll always be greater than the sum of their parts, and in many ways they know it, even if they don't say it. They've always supported each other, been there for each other, and helped each other surmount obstacles from getting a first break to romantic breakups. It doesn't matter that when they've toured they've been on separate buses, or that they now live in different parts of the country. The bond is unbreakable.

So where does it all go? After ten years it's hard to imagine a pop chart that doesn't include OutKast. But for a couple of years yet, that's not going to be a problem. It's going to be left to the future to really assess how much of an influence they've been on music, but on first glance, it's immense. They took hip-hop out of the hands of suburban boys who wanted to imagine themselves as gangstas and gave it to everyone. Probably not since Coolio had anyone made real hip-hop that could be pop music—yet was still very real. It was for all people, old, young, and of every color and creed. It was, in essence, American music in the very best sense.

Most artists these days become massive from the word "go," then struggle to retain or better that status. OutKast has built gradually, stuck to their ideals, and let the music grow gradually. It took them ten years to reach their current status. That's a decade of hard work, of being willing to try new things, of inspiration and sweat. They've fully earned their success and adulation. Much of what they have at the moment might have come from one serendipitous song, but their whole career is full of gems. They could have stayed with the pack and still been reasonably successful. Instead they followed their muses and struck out for unexplored territory.

Hip-hop—and music in general—owes OutKast a debt. They've opened it up, made it joyous, and broken down so many barriers that it'll never be the same again. In an era when everything has been so neatly pigeonholed and categorized, they've scribbled all over the genre markings. And they've done it so well that nobody's cared. They've gained the support of both critics and fans, a rare combination.

There's been nothing manufactured about what they've done; it's all been very palpably their own work. And where they'll take it on the next couple of albums remains every bit as exciting as the work they've done so far.

They've made history, in their own small way. They've created the soundtrack for a number of years for a lot of people, which is perhaps as much as anyone can hope to achieve in music. They've brought pleasure to millions, they've crossed racial and generational barriers, and they've shown a way forward for hip-hop and pop music. Where other big sellers will end up as little more than footnotes in the history of music (and then remembered only for selling so many records), they'll warrant a full entry for their work and its scope.

Big Boi and Andre 3000 have proved to be a combination that's as strong apart as together—when apart actually is together in a way. And they've done it all with grace and sublime, sometimes outrageous style. They've kept it real—and also merrily surreal.

OUTKAST TIMELINE

1975

February 1: Antwan "Big Boi" Patton born in Savannah, Georgia.

May 27: Andre "Dre" Benjamin born in Decatur, Georgia.

1990

Dre goes to live with his father in East Point.

Big Boi and Dre meet at the mall and realize they are both sophomores at Tri-Cities High School. A friendship begins. They start a rap group, 2 Shades Deep, which becomes Misfit, then OutKast.

1992

Big Boi and Dre meet Rico Wade of Organized Noize and begin
    working in his studio.

Dre drops out of high school.

OutKast signs a production deal with Organized Noize.

1993

Once Big Boi and Dre turn eighteen, they sign a record deal
    with Atlanta-based LaFace Records.

"Player's Ball" is released as a Christmas single.

1994

January: "Player's Ball" is reissued, minus the Christmas effect
    of sleigh bells.

The video for "Player's Ball" is directed by Sean "Puffy" Combs.

March: "Player's Ball" sells half a million copies and tops the
    Billboard Hot Rap Singles chart for six weeks.

April: *Southernplayalisticadillacmuzik* is released and goes gold by
    June, even as "Player's Ball" cracks the Top 40.

September:"Git Up, Git Out" is released as a single.

1995

January: OutKast contributes "Phobia" to the soundtrack of the
    movie *Higher Learning*.

OutKast is named Best New Group at the *Source* awards.

April: *Southernplayalisticadillacmuzik* goes platinum.

1996

July: "Elevators (Me & You)" is released.

August: OutKast drops *ATLiens*.

"Elevators (Me & You)" tops the *Billboard* Hot Rap Singles chart and the Hot R&B Singles chart for four weeks.

September: "Elevators (Me & You) sells half a million copies and receives a gold disc.

ATLiens tops the *Billboard* R&B Albums chart for two weeks.

November: Seven Sirius, the child of Dre and Erykah Badu, is born.

November: *ATLiens* goes platinum.

1997

"ATLiens" and "Jazzy Belle" are both released as singles.

1998

August: "Rosa Parks" is released.

September: OutKast releases *Aquemini*.

November: *Aquemini* receives platinum certification.

1999

February: OutKast receives their first Grammy Award, for Best Rap Performance by a Duo or Group, for "Rosa Parks."

Cool Breeze, also members of the Dungeon family, tops the *Billboard* Rap Singles chart with "Watch for the Hook," helped by OutKast.

July: *Aquemini* goes double platinum.

November: Rosa Parks's suit against OutKast over the use of her name in their song is dismissed in Michigan.

OutKast begins recording their new album at their own Stankonia Studios in Atlanta.

2000

September: "B.O.B." is released.

October: *Stankonia* finally arrives in stores after its release date has been put back several times.

November: *Stankonia* reaches double platinum status.

December: "Ms. Jackson" tops the *Billboard* R&B/Hip-hop Singles chart for two weeks and the Hip-hop/R&B Airplay chart for six weeks.

2001

January: "Ms. Jackson" reaches the Top 40.

February: "Ms. Jackson" goes to number one on the Top 40 for a week, also topping the Hot Rap Singles chart for three weeks.

June: "So Fresh, So Clean" makes the Top 40.

OutKast contributes "Speedballin' " to the soundtrack of *Tomb Raider*.

September: OutKast takes home an MTV Video Music Award for Best Hip-hop video for "Ms. Jackson."

November: OutKast is nominated for five Grammy Awards.

December: The greatest hits collection, *Big Boi & Dre Present . . . OutKast*, arrives in stores just in time for Christmas. It includes three previously unreleased tracks. *Billboard* names OutKast Top R&B/Hip-hop Album Artists in their year-end chart.

2002

January: "The Whole World" by OutKast featuring Killer Mike is released.

February: "The Whole World" hits the Top 40.

OutKast goes home with two Grammy Awards, for Best Rap Performance by a Duo or Group for "Ms. Jackson" and Best Rap Album for *Stankonia*.

March: *Big Boi & Dre Present . . . OutKast* is certified platinum.

OutKast wins the World Music Award for World's Best-selling Rap Group.

June: OutKast wins Best Group at the BET Awards.

August: "The Whole World" is nominated for Best Hip-hop Video in the MTV Video Music Awards. It doesn't win.

October: The *GQ* Men of the Year Awards names OutKast Band Men of the Year.

2003

January: OutKast wins an American Music Award as Favorite Hip-hop/R&B Band/Duo/Group.

February: Dre and Big Boi pick up a Grammy for "The Whole World," voted Best Rap Performance by a Duo or Group.

June: Music channel VH1 includes "Ms. Jackson" at #81 in the 100 Best Songs of the Past 25 Years; additionally, OutKast comes in at #21 on the channel's 50 Greatest Hip-hop Artists list.

Seven years after its release, *ATLiens* finally notches up to double platinum status.

September: "Hey Ya!" is released as a single and crashes into the Top 40.

Speakerboxxx/The Love Below hits stores. It immediately tops the *Billboard* Album chart and the R&B/Hip-hop Album chart.

October: Within a month of its release, *Speakerboxxx/The Love Below* sells three million copies.

November: "Hey Ya!" climbs to number one and stays there for seven weeks.

The simultaneously released "The Way You Move" goes into the Top 40.

Both *Stankonia* and *Speakerboxxx/The Love Below* reach the four
million in sales mark.

OutKast is nominated for six Grammy Awards.

December: "Hey Ya!" rests atop four different charts, while
"The Way You Move" goes to number two on the Top 40 and
to the pole position on the *Billboard* Hot Rap Tracks chart.

2004

January: "The Way You Move" takes over the number-one spot
on the Top 40 from "Hey Ya!" and stays there for six weeks,
while "Hey Ya!" achieves number one in Canada.

Speakerboxxx/The Love Below is certified as eight times platinum.

February: "The Way You Move" tops three different charts.

OutKast is awarded Grammys for Album of the Year, Urban/
Alternative Performance of the Year (for "Hey Ya!"), and Best
Rap Album.

March: *Speakerboxxx/The Love Below* reaches nine times platinum.

Andre 3000 films the part of Dabu in *Be Cool*, the sequel to *Get
Shorty*.

May: OutKast begins filming a movie for HBO Productions.

DISCOGRAPHY

The Way You Move (reached #1, 2004)

Roses (2004)

ALBUMS

Southernplayalistcadillacmuzik (April 1994, reached #20)

Peaches (Intro) • Myintroroletuknow • Ain't No Thang • Welcome to Atlanta (Interlude) • Southerplayalisticadillacmuzik • Call of Da Wild • Player's Ball (Original) • Claimin' True • Funky Ride • Flim Flam (Interlude) • Git Up, Git Out • True Dat (Interlude) • Deep • Crumblin' Erb • Hootie Hoo • Player's Ball (Reprise)

ATLiens (August 1996, reached #2)

You May Die (Intro) • Two Dope Boyz (in a Cadillac) • ATLiens • Wheelz of Steel • Jazzy Belle • Elevators (Me & You) • Ova Da Wudz • Babylon • Wailin' • Mainstream • Decatur Psalm • Millennium • E.T. (Extraterrestrial) • 13th Floor/Growing Old • Elevators (Me & You) [ONP 86 Mix]

Aquemini (September 1998, reached #2)

Hold On, Be Strong • Return of the "G" • Rosa Parks • Skew It on the Bar-B (with Raekwon) • Aquemini • Synthesizer (with George Clinton) • Slump • West Savannah • Da Art of Storytellin' (Part 1) • Da Art of Storytellin' (Part 2) • Mamacita • Spottieottiedopaliscious • Y'All Scared (with Big Gipp, T-Mo, and Khujo) • Nathaniel • Liberation • Chonkyfire

Stankonia (October 2000, reached #2)

Intro • Gasoline Dreams (with Khujo Goodie) • I'm Cool (Interlude) • So Fresh, So Clean • Ms. Jackson • Snappin' & Trappin' (with Killer Mike and J-Sweat) • D.F. (Interlude) • Spaghetti

Junction • Kim & Cookie (Interlude) • I'll Call Before I Come (with Gangster Boo & Eco) • B.O.B. [Bombs Over Baghdad] • Xplosion (with B-Real) • We Luv Deez Hoez (with Backbone and Big Gipp) • Humble Mumble (with Erykah Badu) • Drinking Again (Interlude) • ? • Red Velvet • Cruisin' in the ATL (Interlude) • Gangsta Sh*t (with Slim Calhoun) • Toilet Tisha • Slum Beautiful (with Cee-Lo) • Pre-Nump (Interlude) (with Big Rube and Sleepy Brown) • Stankonia [Stanklove]

Big Boi & Dre Present . . . OutKast
(December 2001, reached #18)

Intro • Funkin' Around • Ain't No Thang • So Fresh, So Clean • Rosa Parks • The Whole World (with Killer Mike) • Aquemini • B.O.B. [Bombs Over Baghdad] • Southernplayalisticadillacmuzik • Crumblin' Erb • Ms. Jackson • Player's Ball (Original) • Elevators (Me & You) • Spottieottiedopaliscious • Git Up, Git Out • Movin' Cool (the After Party)

Speakerboxxx/The Love Below (September 2003, reached #1)

DISC ONE: The Love Below (Intro) • Love Hater • God (Interlude) • Happy Valentine's Day • Spread • Where Are My Panties? • Prototype • She Lives in My Lap • Hey Ya! • Roses • Good Day, Good Sir • Behold a Lady • Pink & Blue • Love in War • She's Alive • Dracula's Wedding • My Favorite Things • Take Off Your Cool (with Norah Jones) • Vibrate • A Life in the Day of Benjamin Andre (Incomplete) • [Untitled Hidden Track]

DISC TWO: Intro • Ghetto Musick • Unhappy • Bowtie • The Way You Move • The Rooster • Bust (with Killer Mike) • War • Church • Bamboo (Interlude) • Tomb of the Boom (with Ludacris) • E-Mac (Interlude) • Knowing • Flip Flop

Rock (with Killer Mike) • Interlude • Reset • D-Boi (Interlude) • Last Call (with Slimm Calhoun) • Bowtie (Postlude)

VIDEOS

OutKast Uncovered (2002)

acknowledgments

The act of writing might be solitary, but all around it are the contributions of many others. I'm grateful, as always, to Madeleine Morel, an agent who's worth her weight in gold. To Michael Connor at St. Martin's Press, for believing in the idea. To Kevan Roberts, thanks for the loan of the album (you will get it back). The Leeds United e-mail list, for providing distraction and entertainment when most needed. To (Queen) Suzie 314, for knowledge. To my mother, Betty, for her constant encouragement. To Pepper, simply for being there, and to Mardi, Silvi, Jess, and Esme. To Linda and Graham, of course, for tolerance— although by now they're used to it. And to family and friends whose support is always there: Kevin, Jonathan, Thom, Jim,

Richard, and all the others who've wished me well with the project.

A great deal of material forms the background to this book, and I'm grateful to the following pieces:

"Rap's OutKast, Better Heard than Seen," by David Segal, *The Washington Post*; "OutKast Proves It's No Johnny-Come-Lately," by Soren Baker, *Los Angeles Times*; "Rappers Who Definitely Know How to Rock," by Kelefa Sanneh, *The New York Times*; "Rappers Turn Dialectic into a Conversation," by Jon Pareles, *The New York Times*; "Kast Party," by Ken Tucker, *Entertainment Weekly*; "So Superfunkyfragelistic! On the Edge with the Weird and Wonderful OutKast," by Lorraine Ali, *Newsweek*; "OutKast," by Dimitri Ehrlich, *Interview*; "Rap duo OutKast Stays True to Its Roots," author unknown, *The Oak Ridger*; "Puttin' Some Stank on It," by Billy Johnson, Jr., *Launch.com*; "OutKast Big Boi on 'Bombs Over Baghdad'—Free Music," by Aimee Deep; "The Pride of Funkenstein," by Rob Brunner, *Entertainment Weekly*; Interview, author unknown, NME; Interview, author unknown, *Soul Train*; "OutKast Struts Its Stuff," Brenda Lloyd, *Daily News Record*; "OutKast Hones Their Hip-hop to an Edge," by Errol Nazareth, *Toronto Sun*; "OutKast Is on the Inside Track," by Alex White, publication unknown; "The Inside Story on Hip-hop's Outsiders," by Cheo Hodari Coker, *Los Angeles Times*; "Erykah Badu," by Clarence Waldron, *Jet*; "OutKast 'Aquemini'" by Cheo Tyehimba, *Entertainment Weekly*; "What the Fuss Is About," by Dumisani Ndlovu, *The Music Monitor*; "Joint Effort," by Tony Ware, *Baltimore City Paper*; "OutKast in the Promised Land," by Miles Marshall Lewis, publication unknown; "Buy the OutKast CD and Catch the Sale on Dogs and Paintings," by Chris Nerlson, *The New York Times*; "OutKast: Aliens in Cadillacs," author unknown,

Mic Check; "OutKast: In Through the Out Door," author unkown, *VH1.com*; "Bitches and Money," by Andrew Beaujon, *Spin*; "OutKast—Looking Fresh," by had, *Sixshot.com*; "OutKast makes it mainstream," by Robert Hilburn, *Los Angeles Times*; "OutKast, Rap's Odd Couple: Gangsta Meets Granola," by Lola Ogunnaike, *The New York Times*; "OutKast," by Marti Yarbrough, *Jet*; "Let Their Freak Funk Fly," by Anthony Brozza, *Rolling Stone*; "The Funk Soul Brothers," by Mark Binelli, *Rolling Stone*; "Faraway, So Close," by Jon Caramanica, *MTV Magazine*; "Dre Talks OutKast Projects," Anthony Bozza, *Rolling Stone*; "What Are OutKast Listening to?" author unknown, *MTV.com*; "OutKast Extends Helping Hand," by Gail Mitchell, *Billboard*; "OutKast, author unknown," *Teen People*; "Erykah Badu Gives Birth," author unknown, *Jet*; "Dynamic Duo," by Ethan Brown, *New York Metro*; "OutKast," by Joseph Patel, *Complex*; "Southern Swelter," by Joe Silva, *Musicedge.com*; "Southern-fried Hip-hop," author unknown, *Ebony*; "When Rap sounds anything but Urban," by Jon Caramanica, *The New York Times*; "OutKast: Music's Favorite Odd Couple," by Marti Yarbrough, *Jet*; "Atlanta, GA," by Jeff Clark, *Billboard*; "Grammy's Fun Couple," by Chuck Arnold/ Kristin Harmel/ Marisa Laudadio/ Laura Downey, *People*; "Dysfunction Junction," by Josh Tyrangiel, *Time*; "Inside OutKast," by Elena Romero, *Daily News Record*; "Speak of the Devil," author unknown, *Entertainment Weekly*; "Ride in the Whirlwind," by Kris Ex, *Los Angeles Times*; "Sweeten the Image, Hold the Bling-bling," by Lola Ogunnaike, *The New York Times*; "Atypical OutKast Grammy Bound," author unknown, Associated Press; "OutKast Double the Funk," by Kathy McCabe, *The Daily Telegraph*, Sydney, Australia; "OutKast: Two Is the Magic Number," by Brian Ives & C. Bottomley, *VH1.com*; "OutKast tekk a 'West Side Story'" by

Corey Moss, *VH1.com*; "OutKast," by Nichole Beattie-Rapaport, *Interview*; "Twins Beneath the Skin," by Allison Samuels, *Newsweek*; "Of Two Minds," by Toure, *Rolling Stone*; "One Half of OutKast Speaks Out," by Alex Petridis, *Mail & Guardian*; " 'Speakerboxxx/The Love Below,' " by Chuck Arnold, *People*; " 'Speakerboxxx/The Love Below,' " by Rashaun Hall, *Billboard*.